COLLECTIVE SPIRIT, CONCRETE ACTION

'This book marking the landmark 100th episode of *Mann Ki Baat* is a record of the nation's developmental journey with Modi ji, since the first episode was aired in October 2014. It features a host of interesting nuggets covering diverse fields, culling out inspirational stories about unsung heroes and agents of change across this vast nation. The book documents fascinating facets of Prime Minister Narendra Modi's ongoing conversations with 1.3 billion people of the world's largest democracy, celebrating change-makers and grassroots champions, bringing about societal change in a silent, inspiring manner. While highlighting an array of social, economic, environmental, cultural, health and fitness issues of pressing significance featured in *Mann Ki Baat*, this book also provides us a glimpse into Prime Minister Modi's untiring efforts to educate, guide and motivate our countrymen to strive towards pervasive social change and national development while focussing on their communities. *Collective Spirit, Concrete Action* not only has immense historical value for these reasons, but also helps us to comprehend the dreams of a nation which is fast rising on the international stage as a major global player.'

—M. Venkaiah Naidu
Former Vice President of India

COLLECTIVE SPIRIT, CONCRETE ACTION

Mann Ki Baat **and Its Influence on India**

SHASHI SHEKHAR

RUPA

Published by
Rupa Publications India Pvt. Ltd 2023
7/16, Ansari Road, Daryaganj
New Delhi 110002

Sales centres:
Prayagraj Bengaluru Chennai
Hyderabad Jaipur Kathmandu
Kolkata Mumbai

P-ISBN: 978-93-5702-096-1

First impression 2023

10 9 8 7 6 5 4 3 2 1

The moral right of the author has been asserted.

Printed in India

To the Hon'ble Prime Minister of India
Shri Narendra Modi

CONTENTS

FOREWORD

Mann Ki Baat is a unique exercise of bonding between Prime Minister (PM) Narendra Modi and the people of India. As he completes a full century of those talks, its multiple dimensions and purposes become more apparent.

Call it a social revolution, an innovative outreach programme, a monthly dose of inspiration or a progress report to the nation, the PM's social contact programme is an imaginative utilization of a century-old medium by one of the most tech-savvy politicians of our era. Indeed, whether it is the comfort of the listeners or the musings of his heart, this endeavour highlights his deep understanding of the mindset of 140 crore Indians. That he has diligently met this commitment now for more than 100 months speaks of his passion for dialogue with the people. And that they equally devotedly tune in to *Mann Ki Baat*, underlines their expectations of him.

The last few years have presented several challenges, none as daunting as the Covid-19 pandemic. In the face of this, *Mann Ki Baat* exhorted us all towards *janbhagidari*. The people of India found both courage and strength in the thoughts that their leader shared with them so openly. Whether it was to educate on social distancing—*Do gaz ki doori; Mask hai zaroori*—or encouraging the vaccination drive—*Dawai bhi; Kadai bhi*—it was the PM's direct messaging that helped the nation tide over a once-in-a-century challenge.

The belief in *janshakti* extended to opportunities as much as to challenges. Nowhere was it more evident than in the exhortation to take forward the most sweeping solution to a perennial shortage that India has faced—that of water. Citing examples that range from Vellore to Srinagar and Jalore to Meghalaya, the merits of water conservation, river revival, rainwater harvesting and Amrit Sarovar entered mass consciousness. The water-warrior joined the Covid-warrior in popular lexicon.

As India enters the Amrit Kaal—an era of national rejuvenation—PM Modi reignited interest in Indian heroes by launching campaigns on freedom struggle in different languages; announcing competitions on patriotic songs, rangolis and loris; and seeking from people their ideas for the Tiranga campaign. In tandem, he relentlessly promoted *atmanirbharta* as a habit as much as a policy. *Mann Ki Baat* was a game changer in spreading the message of 'Vocal for Local,' with examples across multiple domains to which the ordinary citizen related. One visible outcome of these efforts was the revival of the Indian toy industry. Atmanirbharta is a mindset, and its expressions range across all aspects of human activity. It was, therefore, only natural that there be a sustained focus on grassroots-level champions in various walks of life. From a Moradabad example of slipper manufacturing to making masks with Madhubani motifs, the discourse went on to cover maintaining cooking traditions in Sambalpur and hoisting the tricolour by our divyang brethren at Siachen glacier.[1]

Nature and environment have been powerful themes of *Mann Ki Baat*, including the contribution of the youth. Campaigning against single-use plastic was an early focus that was followed by catching the rain, repairing river banks, protecting sparrows and waterfalls and worshipping the sun. The next-gen was connected to these goals by technology and innovation efforts in this direction. It could be the growing number of Unicorns, the contribution of artificial intelligence (AI), plogging exercises or beautification by students. Sports, too, were given the required salience by a PM who has so strongly propagated Khelo India and Fit India. He shed light on individual achievements and ongoing events as much as on motivational figures and a healthy lifestyle.

A society that is in the midst of national rejuvenation is understandably inspired by a reminder of its history, culture and traditions. In the course of these 100 episodes, a vast range of experiences, personalities and happenings have featured in the ruminations that the PM has shared with the country. They could be about history—from Lord Basaveshwara and Adi Shankaracharya to Guru Nanak Dev Ji and Maharishi Valmiki. Sometimes, more contemporary figures like Bhagwan Birsa Munda and Swami Vivekananda were invoked as inspiration. The importance of heritage, too, was brought out by demonstrating the relevance of our scriptures to current challenges. The sacrifices of preceding generations, be it the war of independence or more recent conflicts, emerged as a powerful reminder of our national spirit. The achievements of today's India found equally regular mention so that the entire nation could celebrate its talent and creativity.

---

[1]Please see Chapter 12, 'From Cradle to Communities', for a detailed discussion on the use of the word 'divyang'.

From the perspective of foreign policy, *Mann Ki Baat* has been an extraordinary vehicle to connect our citizens to the world. On occasion, complex diplomatic activities have been demystified and put across by PM Modi in everyday language. I can remember, for example, the ASEAN heads of State and government being the subject of a talk in March 2018. By associating with the significance of the Ramayana in their particular societies, a link was built with the average Indian. Similarly, on the United Nations (UN) Day 2021, the PM spoke of the role played by Indian women in advancing that body's influence. While referring to India's different associations with the UN, he also recalled PM Vajpayee's 1977 UN address in Hindi.

Sometimes, global initiatives have been similarly explained by the PM in a simple but effective manner. A recent example was in congratulating the country at the end of 2022 on taking up the presidency of the G20. He urged that it should be approached as a mass endeavour in the true spirit of janbhagidari. Early this year, he focussed on the International Year of Millets that India has so strongly campaigned for and is currently advocating. Yoga has been a subject of multiple discussions over the last many years. References have ranged from the manner of practice to individual practitioners.

Given the greater respect accorded by the Modi government to the Indian diaspora, it is also natural that they be the subject of some episodes. A prominent case was that pertaining to President Chandrikapersad Santokhi of Suriname, who took his oath of office starting with a Vedic hymn. It need not always be such high-profile events; quite often, the activities of the Indian community abroad in the course of its daily life have also merited attention. *Mann Ki Baat* has heard stories of practitioners of

Indian martial arts abroad, the celebration of our festivals and the observance of our traditions.

Understandably, all Indians feel proud when those of other nations contribute to our heritage and advance our culture. But in most cases, the average citizen is not even aware of such happenings. Prime Minister Modi has heightened awareness in this regard by highlighting specific cases in various domains. Notable among them are the teaching of Bhagavad Gita in Brazil, a Mahabharata project in Japan, the propagation of khadi in Mexico, the popularization of our music in Tanzania and Greece and the translation of ancient Indian texts in Mongolia.

There have been occasions of emotional connect between India and our partners abroad in recent years. The example that I personally identify with pertains to the handing over of the relics of St Queen Ketevan to the government and people of Georgia from their resting place in Goa. I had the privilege of personally taking the relics to that country. A second one relates to PM Modi's appreciation of the inauguration by his Singaporean counterpart of the renovated Silat Road Gurudwara. As a former high commissioner there, it brought back many memories.

As *Mann Ki Baat* approaches its hundredth episode, *Collective Spirit, Concrete Action* delves into the vast array of topics that it has covered to assess the programme's multidimensional impact. The book also examines the various academic efforts analysing the programme to place it within the context of the mass societal changes of the last decade. As a broadcaster, the author has not just been a close observer of the making of *Mann Ki Baat*, but also a witness to its influence far beyond radiowaves, TV screens and mobile phones. Through this book, he has explored the life journeys of the various change-makers featured on *Mann Ki*

Baat to paint a vivid picture of how New India is taking shape. It makes for a compelling read for those keen to understand India's transformational journey.

Dr S. Jaishankar
External Affairs Minister of India and
Member of Parliament (Rajya Sabha) from Gujarat

PREFACE

Mann Ki Baat, the monthly radio programme hosted by Prime Minister (PM) Narendra Modi since October 2014, is a unique platform for the leader of the world's largest democracy to converse directly with the citizens of India and share his thoughts on various issues of national and global importance. This programme, inviting listeners to share their feedback, suggestions and stories with the PM through various channels, has covered a wide range of topics such as social welfare, education, health, environment, culture, sports, science and technology, foreign policy and national security.

While *Mann Ki Baat* has been the subject of two earlier books and several studies, this exploration of the programme, from October 2014 to March 2023, as it nears its hundredth episode, is focussed on many inspiring examples of ordinary people who have made extraordinary contributions to society in different fields and have seen their efforts be amplified through the programme. In addition to offering insight into the vision and values that have informed *Mann Ki Baat*, this book also reflects on the deep connection of the people of India with its culture, history and languages.

Mann Ki Baat stands out with its focus on grassroots impact. By promoting various initiatives aimed at empowering citizens and improving their well-being, the programme has turned India's development into a collective movement. It has effectively generated awareness and rallied public support for a range of social causes, including cleanliness, water conservation, digital literacy, yoga, organ donation, road safety and women's empowerment. Additionally, the programme has inspired individuals to adopt positive habits such as reading, playing games, learning new skills and celebrating festivals in an eco-friendly way.

Another remarkable aspect of *Mann Ki Baat* is its portrayal of India's developmental journey through the eyes of PM Modi. The programme highlights the nation's triumphs over numerous challenges and its accomplishments in fields such as economy, infrastructure, energy, healthcare, education, space, defence, diplomacy, and culture over the past nine years. It offers insights into India's potential to become a global leader in the twenty-first century.

PROLOGUE

How do you have a conversation with a billion-strong democracy? How do you converse with its boundless aspirations, myriad dreams, multitude of challenges, collage of emotions and orchestra of expressions? How do you listen to the pulse of the nation and feel its heartbeat? How do you motivate change while being the change itself? How do you celebrate agents of change while persuading many more to join their ranks? How do you look to the past for inspiration while creating hope for a better future? How do you nurture the spirit of innovation, industry and enterprise while deepening the bond with Nature? How do you call for action to combat climate change while securing the food chain? How do you hold a dialogue from the heart with a billion hearts, minds and souls, month after month, year after year?

Collective Spirit, Concrete Action is more than just the chronicle of a radio programme. It captures an evolving conversation that navigates India's present, learns from its past and shapes its future. This book unveils how a glimmer of hope has pierced the shadows of cynicism, revealing the power of people-driven social change. It brings to life the inspiring stories of change-makers who, against all odds, have transformed everyday lives in their communities, and how these communities have united to generate a wave of change.

The book highlights endeavours to harmonize technology and nature, creating a more sustainable world. It narrates the tale of a nation, driven by its leader, uniting for the greater good. The book provides a window into how children have been inspired to envision a brighter future and become agents of change themselves. It showcases the potency of words, metaphors, languages and creative expressions in preserving culture, conserving the environment and promoting innovation and enterprise.

Collective Spirit, Concrete Action takes the reader through the lives of farmers, the Earth's caretakers, providers, healers, caregivers, first responders and courageous heroes in uniform. It commemorates emotional moments and celebrates monumental achievements in sports and various fields, in the pursuit of glory.

As PM Narendra Modi's *Mann Ki Baat* approaches its hundredth episode, *Collective Spirit, Concrete Action* delves into the vast array of topics in the programme that have spurred massive societal change. The book explores the various rhetorical tools used in *Mann Ki Baat* to educate, inspire, motivate and guide citizens. Engaging with both change-makers and decision-makers, it evaluates the programme's real-world impact beyond radio waves. The book also chronicles academic efforts analysing multiple aspects of *Mann Ki Baat* and delves into the making of each episode, examining its ever-growing reach across India's diverse linguistic landscape. By placing key moments from the programme, within the larger context of India's developmental journey over the past nine years, *Collective Spirit, Concrete Action* seeks to unravel the thought process underpinning PM Narendra Modi's *Mann Ki Baat*.

CHAPTER 1

THE SINGLE THREAD OF NATIONAL PURPOSE

W hen poet, Nobel laureate and polymath Gurudev Rabindranath Tagore penned 'Bharoto Bhagyo Bidhata' (dispenser of India's destiny) back in 1911, little did he know that half a century later, its first stanza, 'Jana Gana Mana' (people, communities, minds), would go on to define an independent, democratic India. While the Constituent Assembly adopted 'Jana Gana Mana' as the national anthem in 1950, Netaji Subhas Chandra Bose had declared it as the anthem for a free India in 1941 itself. Lyrically traversing the geography of India, 'Jana Gana Mana' is a mirror to the linguistic diversity of India. It was at this intersection of geography and linguistic diversity that the design of Indian federalism was envisioned by yet another icon of modern India, Dr B.R. Ambedkar. His vision was one of an indivisible union of states within the single framework of the Indian Constitution, with flexibility built in. Translating this design of the Indian Union into reality was a task for yet another great son of India, Sardar Vallabhbhai Patel, India's first home minister and deputy PM, popularly known as the Iron Man of India. Connecting the dots from Tagore's creative genius to Ambedkar's progressivism and Patel's grit and determination, PM Narendra Modi's *Mann Ki Baat* is, in many ways, the story of India's federalism over the past 75 years.

Prime Minister Modi's ascent as India's PM back in 2014 was the first time a sitting chief minister (CM) contested and campaigned in the general election as a party's PM candidate. His path to the highest office in India was unlike any of his predecessors. While Jawaharlal Nehru, India's first PM was Mahatma Gandhi's preferred candidate, his successor Lal Bahadur Shastri was already serving in Nehru's cabinet as a Union minister. Nehru's daughter Indira Gandhi and grandson Rajiv Gandhi had no experience in running a state government, and other non-Congress PMs were mostly Delhi-based politicians of various political parties. The lone exception to this list is H.D. Deve Gowda, who, in 1996 was serving as the CM of Karnataka. In Gowda's case, however, he was parachuted to Delhi after the 1996 General Election as a compromise candidate of an unwieldy coalition of regional parties.

Prime Minister Modi was the first to not only make the transition from the chief executive of a state to the Centre but to do so leading from the front, as both the declared leader of the Bharatiya Janata Party (BJP) and as its candidate for the Lok Sabha from both Vadodara and Varanasi. In his journey from Gujarat to New Delhi, he traversed more than 25 states, addressing hundreds of campaign events across the length and breadth of India while immersing himself in the rich diversity of its various states, experiencing the myriad dialects, cultures and landscapes. Some distinctive features of his campaign speeches were greetings to the teeming crowds in the local dialect; invocation of local icons and symbols; quotes from local poets; and tributes to local heroes.

These were no election gimmicks or stray references. Prime Minister Modi's mind was already working on how to weave the diverse socio-cultural fibres that run across the states into a single thread of national purpose. When he announced his radio programme, *Mann Ki Baat*, in October 2014, less than six months into office as PM, he was acutely aware of the challenges of engaging citizens across India. From invoking the collective strength of 1.25 crore Indians to harking back to his tenure as the CM of Gujarat, his first radio broadcast was a curtain-raiser on how sustaining a national dialogue would require him to simultaneously talk to the east, listen to the west, reach out to the north and immerse himself in the south.

BRIDGING MANY DIVIDES

Central to PM Modi's efforts to weave a national thread and bring together the diversity of states in India, has been his formulation of Ek Bharat Shreshtha Bharat (One India, Best India [EBSB]). Drawing inspiration from his role model, Sardar Patel, PM Modi unveiled his thinking behind EBSB during the *Mann Ki Baat* episode of October 2015, ahead of Sardar Patel's birth anniversary, which is also celebrated as National Unity Day. Speaking further on this idea of unity in diversity across Indian states, he emphasized how celebrating diversity was key to ensuring peace and harmony in society.

Since PM Modi's articulation of EBSB in 2015, the idea has taken a life of its own across states, schools, universities and youth initiatives. If the EBSB is a government-sponsored campaign to some, to others, it is yet another Modi-nym, adding to the long vocabulary of acronyms that have come to be identified with the PM. While there have been a large number of public events organized under the banner of EBSB over the past nine years, the true impact of EBSB on the psyche of Indian citizens can be assessed via the personal experiences of cultural intermingling resulting in lasting bonds and indelible memories. With students from far-west Bundi in Rajasthan learning Assamese to lessons in Haryanvi being delivered in Telangana, PM Modi's EBSB experiment has inched towards becoming a mass movement of sorts. It has motivated students from mountainous Himachal Pradesh to trek all the way down to the backwaters of Kerala to learn the secrets of making piping hot and spicy sambar; it has deepened an appreciation for the Northeast in students from Madhya Pradesh, spending time in the interiors of Nagaland.

A fine example of this mass experiment bridging linguistic divides can be found in the experiences of a student group from Patiala in Punjab, that not only learned Telugu but developed adequate fluency to extend greetings and express gratitude at events hosted in their honour in Andhra Pradesh.[1] Moreover, with over 16 spoken languages on campus, the Indian Institute of Technology (IIT) Jodhpur is also representative of the breadth of diversity that EBSB attempts to bridge.[2]

---

[1]Jagga, Raakhi, 'Cultural Exchange: Punjabi Students Learn Telugu, Bond with Andhra Counterparts Over Food, Music, Dance', *The Indian Express*, 15 July 2022, https://tinyurl.com/2f874e8h. Accessed on 10 April 2023.

[2]Gupta, Riddhima, 'At IIT Jodhpur Campus 16 Languages Are Spoken: Survey', *News18*, 6 October 2022, https://tinyurl.com/42m4jmb4. Accessed on 10 April 2023.

Seeking to find unity in India's linguistic diversity, *Mann Ki Baat* sourced an innovative idea for EBSB from two Tanzanian siblings, Kili Paul and his sister, Neema. The siblings created a buzz on Facebook, Twitter and Instagram because of their passion for Indian music, which earned them transcontinental popularity. A video of Kili lip-syncing 'Jana Gana Mana' on the occasion of Republic Day went viral on social media. A soulful tribute to Lata Mangeshkar by lip-syncing her song earned the siblings a mention on *Mann Ki Baat* for their creativity, apart from being honoured at the Indian Embassy in Tanzania. Noting how Indian music has fascinated performers across the globe, PM Modi recalled how a few years ago, singers and musicians from more than 150 countries participated in a video compilation, where they sang 'Vaishnava Jana To', Mahatma Gandhi's favourite hymn, in their respective national dresses.

Today, when India is celebrating the important festival of 75th year of its Independence, similar initiatives can be carried out regarding patriotic songs, wherein foreign nationals or famous singers from abroad are invited to render Indian patriotic songs. Not only this, if Kili and Neema in Tanzania can lip sync the songs of India in this manner, aren't there many types of songs in my country... in many languages of our country... can't any Gujarati children do that with Tamil songs....Some children of Kerala could do that with Assamese songs.... Some Kannadiga children could [do] that with songs of Jammu and Kashmir! We can create such an environment in which we will be able to experience 'Ek Bharat-Shreshtha Bharat'. [...] I urge the youth of the country to make videos of the popular songs of Indian languages in their own way.... You will become very popular! And the diversity of the country will be introduced to the new generation.[3]

Language, however, is not the only dimension in PM Modi's conception of EBSB. When journalists from Punjab were exposed to the traditional handmade wooden toys of Kondapalli in Andhra Pradesh, it was not only an exercise in cultural appreciation but an eye-opener on the many efforts at preservation of local arts and crafts as a heritage.[4]

During his radio address of July 2022, PM Modi, while invoking the spirit of EBSB, stressed on yet another thread of commonality across states—tribal festivals and, more specifically, festivals centred on a female deity:

> Friends, there are many traditional fairs of tribal societies in different states in our country. Some of these fairs are associated with tribal culture, while some are organized in connection with tribal history and heritage. For example, if you get a chance, you must visit the four-day Samakka-Saralamma Jatara Fair in Medaram, Telangana. This fair is called the Mahakumbh of Telangana. The Saralamma Jatara Mela is celebrated in honour of two tribal women heores—Samakka and Saralamma. It is a big center of faith for the Koya tribal community, not only in Telangana, but also in Chhattisgarh, Maharashtra and Andhra Pradesh. The Maridamma fair in Andhra Pradesh is also a big fair connected with the beliefs of the tribal society. The

[3]"PM's Address in the 86th Episode of "Mann Ki Baat"", *PMIndia*, 27 February 2022, https://tinyurl.com/556j2av6. Accessed on 31 March 2023.
[4]Kumar, Aneesha Sareen, "'Ek Bharat Shreshtha Bharat—Punjab & Andhra Pradesh" Handmade Wooden Toys Carve a Success Story', *Hindustan Times*, 9 September 2022, https://tinyurl.com/32s62zab. Accessed on 10 April 2023.

Maridamma fair runs from Jyeshtha Amavasya to Ashadh Amavasya and the tribal society here associates it with Shakti upasana, worship. Here, in Peddhapuram, East Godavari, there is also a Maridamma temple. Similarly, the people of Garasiya tribe in Rajasthan organize 'Siyawa ka Mela' or 'Mankhan Ro Mela' on Vaishakh Shukla Chaturdashi. [...] There must be many such fairs around you too. In modern times, these old links of the society are very important to strengthen the spirit of 'Ek Bharat Shreshtha Bharat'. Our youth must join them and whenever you go to such fairs.[5]

RESCRIPTING FEDERALISM THE MODI WAY

If EBSB came to symbolize the soft side of PM Modi's federalism, it was his formulation of 'Team India', engaging with the CMs of various states in a variety of formats, that made up for his hard federalism. Speaking on how he broke from tradition by reaching out to CMs, he had this to share in his third episode of *Mann Ki Baat* in December of 2014:

Last week I had the chance to have a meeting with the Chief Ministers of all the states. This tradition has been going on for the past 50–60 years. This time it was organized at the Prime Minister's residence. We started it as a retreat program with no papers, no files and no officers. It was a simple interaction where the Prime Minister and Chief Minister were all the same, seated together like friends. For an hour or two, matters of national concern were seriously discussed

[5]'PM's Address in the 91st Episode of "Mann Ki Baat"', *PMIndia*, 31 July, 2022, https://tinyurl.com/3bsdrfam. Accessed on 31 March 2023.

in a friendly atmosphere. Everyone just poured their hearts
out. There was no political agenda involved. This too was
a memorable experience that I wanted to share with you.[6]

In fact, this outreach to states and CMs across party lines has
been a constant throughout PM Modi's nine years in office.
From lauding efforts taken by Gujarat, Maharashtra and Andhra
Pradesh towards water conservation to calling out by name
Mission Bhagiratha by Telangana, his approach to federalism (as
expressed through his monthly radio address) has consistently
transcended partisan divides. His outreach made no distinction
between small and big states, with even the remotest villages in
the smallest of states earning a mention for their community
efforts at transformation.

It is, however, his emphasis on the Northeast that stands out
repeatedly, starting from the earliest of episodes in 2015:

> Bhavesh Deka from Guwahati has written to me on the North-
> East related issues and problems. I must say that North-East
> people are quite active. I really appreciate that they write about
> a lot of issues. I would like to tell them with great pleasure
> that we have a separate ministry for North-Eastern region.
> During the government of Atal Bihari Vajpayee as our Prime
> Minister, a DONER Ministry called 'Development of North-
> East Region' was formed. After our government was formed,
> the DONER Department took an important decision of not
> staying in Delhi and working from centre for the North-
> East regions? Instead it was decided to send the government

---

[6]'English Rendering of the Text of Prime Minister's "Mann ki Baat" on All India Radio on 14th December 2014', *PMIndia*, https://tinyurl.com/yk38v5j8. Accessed on 31 March 2023.

officials and their team on a seven days camp to North-East states like Nagaland, Arunachal Pradesh, Tripura, Assam and Sikkim. These officials would visit the districts, villages and meet the local government officials and talk to people's representatives and the citizens of those regions. They will listen to their problems and direct the government in taking appropriate measures in solving those problems. This initiative will bring a fruitful result in the near future. The officials who will visit these states would realize the beauty of these states and will feel very determined to work for the development of these states and to fix the problems of these states. When they return with this pledge, they can easily understand the problems of these states even when they reach Delhi. This is a great initiative to go far-off from Delhi to East, and this act is called 'Act East Policy'.[7]

From development to tourism, from culture to agriculture, PM Modi's championing of the Northeast is without a precedent or parallel in independent India's 75 years. His focus on the Northeast has decisively turned the region away from backwardness and separatism towards becoming active participants and significant stakeholders in the economic rise of 'New India'. Moreover, deep cultural bonds are also being forged, which is illustrated by the ASEAN–India music festival tapping into the creative energies of the youth of the Northeast. The festival's second edition took place in 2022.

Chief Minister Himanta Biswa Sarma, who has helmed Assam in recent years and has worked extensively across the Northeast

---

[7]'English Rendering of Prime Minister's "Mann ki Baat" on All India Radio', *PMIndia*, 26 July 2015, https://tinyurl.com/4hhr52bf. Accessed on 31 March 2023.

to bridge fault lines, insists that the impact of *Mann Ki Baat* is immeasurable, given the unprecedented affection and attention showered on the region by PM Modi. He notes how regional nuances have had an amplified effect on the ground, with the example of the all-important issue of conservation of rhinoceri in Assam. He attributes the call to action from the programme for the heightened sense of awareness on conservation and increased vigilance against poaching. With this increased focus on the state, he insists that listening to *Mann Ki Baat* on radio has become a common activity in Assam. The mention of the state's leather products of Hailakandi and other agri products on the programme has been particularly helpful for the farmers, producers and manufacturers looking to export their products. Himanta's assessment is that *Mann Ki Baat* has had a direct bearing on the steady rise in exports from the state of horticulture and agriculture products like Bao rice, Assam lemon and Tezpur litchi, thanks to the wide awareness created by PM Modi. This has played a crucial role in Assam's emergence as the economic gateway to Bangladesh via Chittagong.[8]

With the deep sense of bonding that has been established by PM Modi by championing both individual- and community-led efforts across the Northeast, Himanta sees *Mann Ki Baat* as being vital to the continued integration of the region with the rest of India. It is, thus, no accident that one of PM Modi's few ministerial colleagues to figure prominently on *Mann Ki Baat* was Himanta Sarma's predecessor, Sarbananda Sonowal. In May 2016, in spite of his commitments in Assam, Sonowal went beyond the call of duty to personally motivate sportspersons at the Netaji Subhas National Institute of Sports, Patiala, and earned rare praise on *Mann Ki Baat*.

---

[8]In conversation with the author in March 2023.

Prime Minister Modi's federalism has made a constant effort to find creative workarounds to the partisan political divides across states of India. However, this journey to creatively rescript federalism around his notion of Team India and to give it soul through EBSB has not been without hurdles and obstacles. Competitive federal politics at the state level and the BJP's growing footprint in several states where it had a marginal or no presence a decade back has meant that his outreach is greeted with suspicion and downright hostility. It is to PM Modi's credit that he has insulated his programme from these partisan fissures, never letting competitive state-level politics get in the way of greeting states on their formation days; leveraging the radio platform to mobilize aid in case of floods and other disasters; and taking care to celebrate even the smallest of achievements through his radio programme's nationwide broadcast.

If PM Modi has strengthened India's federalism as the captain of Team India, *Mann Ki Baat*, with its myriad regional flavours, has been the glue that has held its spirit together through the dust and din of India's electoral politics, despite many directions in which India's socio-economic diversity has stretched and tested its durability. A case in point is the renaming of the Chandigarh airport after the revolutionary freedom fighter and martyr, Shaheed Bhagat Singh, which was announced by PM Modi during the September 2022 episode of *Mann Ki Baat*. The announcement elicited a rare public appreciation from Bhagwant Mann, CM of the Aam Aadmi Party (AAP)-ruled Punjab.[9] Such is the expectation from PM Modi's *Mann Ki Baat* that even an embattled Ashok

---

[9]"Bhagwant Mann Welcomes PM Modi's Announcement to Name Chandigarh Airport after Bhagat Singh", *The Tribune*, 25 September 2022, https://tinyurl.com/fd8ycmay. Accessed on 10 April 2023.

Gehlot, CM of the Congress-ruled state of Rajasthan, in May 2022, urged for a call to peace in Rajasthan through the programme, as his administration struggled to maintain law and order after a series of violent communal incidents in his state.[10]

An unintended consequence of celebrating linguistic diversity through *Mann Ki Baat* was the reaction of leaders across the political divide touting their multilingual skills. In December 2020, right after PM Modi had recited a Bengali verse, the irrepressible Mamata Banerjee, CM of West Bengal, went out of her way to list all of the Indian languages in which she was fluent. But he has never let partisanship come in the way of duly crediting states and their governments for their achievements. In his address of June 2018, PM Modi dwelt extensively on the role played by the states in the nationwide roll-out of the Goods and Services Tax (GST), while hailing the states for their sagacity in taking collective decisions through the GST Council.

Taking Ambedkar's flexible federalism to a whole new level with his 'co-operative federalism', PM Modi's outreach to states across India has been multidimensional, thanks to the wide canvas of subjects of *Mann Ki Baat*, with every state celebrating its heroes, iconic locales and myriad festivals. The programme, with the national purpose to strengthen the bond of federalism, has celebrated unsung change-makers from all parts of the country as the nation charts its developmental course to modernity.

---

[10]Mishra, Sachin Kumar, 'Mann Ki Baat: अशोक गहलोत बोले, "मन की बात" में देश में शांति की अपील करें पीएम मोदी', *Jagran*, 29 May 2022, https://tinyurl.com/fh65aa3w. Accessed on 10 April 2023.

CHAPTER 2

NATION ABOVE ALL

Mann Ki Baat has been as much a platform for social change initiatives as it has been a vehicle for nation-building. At pivotal moments over the course of the last nine years, be it moments of triumph or crises, *Mann Ki Baat* has played the roles of both the voice of the nation as well as its conscience. It has not shied away from recalling the turbulent moments of India's history, when the nation had to go to war to defend much more than the territory of India, its ideals and the way of the life it has come to represent.

Commemorating battles and the many warriors who laid down their lives, *Mann Ki Baat* has been at the forefront of keeping the flame of nationalism alive seven decades after Indian independence. From observing Parakram Parv to Kargil Vijay Diwas, India's many battles have become an annual commemoration through *Mann Ki Baat*. If the surgical strike of 2016 was fresh in public memory, so was the Battle of Haji Pir Pass, thanks to exhibitions like Shauryanjali, which kept the memory of the wars of 1960s alive.

Explaining the significance of these commemorations, PM Modi told his listeners:

> If you want to create history, then it is necessary to understand the nuances of the past. History binds us to our roots. If we are detached from our history then the possibilities of creating history comes to an end. This exhibition on valour and gallantry helps us to experience our past. It gives us knowledge about our history. And this is an opportunity to inspire people to sow seeds for creating a new history.[1]

Taking to airwaves in July 2015 to mark Kargil Vijay Diwas, PM Modi spoke of the many sacrifices made by India's brave hearts in uniform. A month later, when India was marking 50 years of the 1965 war with Pakistan, PM Modi recalled former PM Lal Bahadur Shastri's famous exhortation of '*Jai Jawan, Jai Kisan*'. The slogan has since seen science, research and innovation added to it to evolve into '*Jai Jawan, Jai Kisan, Jai Vigyan, Jai Anusandhan*'. The slogan underscores PM Modi's nationalism, which is neither unidimensional nor rooted in narrow parochialism, but is much broader in its spirit and universal in its appeal.

It is, however, the February 2019 episode of *Mann Ki Baat* that stands out for it revealed PM Modi's steely resolve in the face of aggression from across the borders. Recalling the deadly terror attack in Pulwama, Jammu and Kashmir, that took the lives of several men in uniform, he struck a rare note of anger, giving voice to the emotions of crores of Indians:

---

[1]'English Rendering of Text of Prime Minister's "Mann Ki Baat" on All India Radio on 20th September 2015', *PMIndia*, 20 September 2015, https://tinyurl.com/2p8tw3te. Accessed on 7 April 2023.

As a consequence of the Pulwama terror attack and the sacrifice of the brave jawans, people across the country are agonized and enraged. All around, there is a deluge of strong feelings of sympathy for the martyrs and their family members. The outrage that singes your being and mine on account of the terrorizing violence replicates itself in the collective inner psyche' of every citizen of the country; it also echoes in pro-humanity communities of the world, which sincerely believe in humanity.[2]

Prime Minister Modi made a solemn promise to his listeners: to be relentless in the war against terrorism. He praised the armed forces for what he called their unparalleled courage and valour and spoke for the first time of retributive justice to the victims, within a hundred hours of the Pulwama attack. Dwelling at length on the life stories of the martyrs of the attack and the emotions of their surviving family members, PM Modi paid homage to their sacrifice with these words:

The martyrdom of these brave soldiers brought to the fore, through the media, touching, inspiring stories of their kin, which give hope and strength to the entire country. The fortitude displayed by Ram Niranjan ji, father of martyr Ratan Thakur of Bhagalpur, Bihar, in this moment of tribulation is truly inspiring. He has expressed the wish of sending his second son too, to take on the enemy; if need be, he himself would go and fight. The country salutes the indomitable courage of Meena ji, wife of martyr Prasanna Sahu of Jagatsinghpur, Odisha. She has vowed to send her

---

[2]'PM's Mann Ki Baat Programme on All India Radio', *PMIndia*, 24 February 2019, https://tinyurl.com/5n7xjj24. Accessed on 7 April 2023.

only son to join the CRPF. When the mortal remains of martyr Vijay Soren, draped in the tricolour reached Gumla, Jharkhand, his innocent son iterated that he too would join the armed forces. The mettle of this innocent lad is a representative sample of the feelings of each and every child of the nation today. Similar sentiments are coming to the fore in the households of our brave heart martyrs. No martyr, no family is an exception to that.

Whether it be the family of martyr Vijay Maurya of Devariya, the parents of martyr Tilakraj of Kangra or the six-year-old son of martyr Hemraj of Kota—the story of every family of martyrs is full of inspiration. I urge the young generation to know and understand the fortitude and the sentiment displayed by these families. To understand the virtues of patriotism, sacrifice and perseverance, one doesn't need to revert to historical events. These are but living examples before your eyes... these very examples are a source of inspiration for the future of a rising and glowing India.[3]

It is a testament to this spirit of nationalism that many widows of servicemen have volunteered to join the armed forces over the years. Prime Minister Modi introduced two of these brave daughters of India to the listeners: Lieutenants Swati Mahadik and Nidhi Dubey of the Indian Army. Recalling the contributions and sacrifices by their late husbands, he recounted the circumstances that saw Swati, the wife of martyred Colonel Santosh Mahadik, join the Indian Army. He also paid tribute to Naik Mukesh Dubey, who died of cardiac arrest, and spoke of Nidhi's resolve to serve the nation.

---

[3]Ibid.

SENTINELS ON EVERY FRONT

The valour of Indian soldiers goes beyond securing the country's borders. Martyrs of World Wars and heroes who laid down their lives while keeping peace in other countries—*Mann Ki Baat* has been both a commemoration and a celebration of these heroes. While marking the centenary of the Battle of Haifa in Israel, PM Modi paid tribute to the brave soldiers of Mysuru (earlier Mysore), Hyderabad and Jodhpur Lancers who had freed Haifa.

With more than 18,000 Indian security personnel having lent their services in United Nations (UN) Peacekeeping operations, PM Modi recalled the sacrifices and contributions of Captain Gurbachan Singh Salaria in Congo, the only Indian soldier to receive the highest gallantry award of Param Vir Chakra while serving as a UN Peacekeeper. In the episode where PM Modi praised the roles of General K.S. Thimayya (Padma Bhushan, Distinguished Service Order) in Cyprus and Lt General Dewan Prem Chand in the breakaway Congo province of Katanga and Cyprus, and later in Namibia, while in his seventies, listeners were also informed about the 7,000 Indian soldiers associated with UN Peacekeeping initiatives—the third highest number of soldiers from any country.

Till August 2017, Indian soldiers had lent their services in about 50 of the total of 71 Peacekeeping operations undertaken by the UN the world over. These operations had been carried out in the Korean peninsula, Cambodia, Laos, Vietnam, Congo, Cyprus, Liberia, Lebanon, Sudan and many other parts of the world. In Congo and South Sudan, more than 20,000 patients were treated in Indian Army hospitals and countless lives were saved. Breaking barriers, India was also the first country to send an all-female Formed Police Unit (FPU) to Liberia for the UN Peace Mission, a pioneering gesture that was soon emulated by other nations.

The valour of Indian soldiers transcends the nation's borders. Yet, India did not have a National War Memorial to commemorate the sacrifices of these brave hearts until recently. This caused much anguish to the PM, and he resolved that the country must have such a memorial. In February 2019, he took to airwaves to present the first National War Memorial to his listeners across India. Dedicating the memorial to the nation, he painted a vivid picture with his words. Located in the close vicinity of India Gate and Amar Jawan Jyoti, the memorial's design, according to PM Modi, symbolized the indomitable courage of immortal soldiers. It consists of four concentric circles, depicting the journey of a soldier from his or her formative training to ultimately culminate in the most supreme of sacrifices on the battlefield. Listeners were treated to a walk from the central flame of the Amar Chakra, symbolizing the immortality of the martyred soldiers. They were then taken through the second circle, the Veerta Chakra, depicting the courage and bravery of the soldiers, which also houses a gallery whose walls are inscribed with soldiers' tales of valour. He then moved to the Tyag Chakra (which stands for the sacrifice of the soldiers), where the names of soldiers who made the supreme sacrifice are inscribed in letters of gold and then to the Rakshak Chakra, which depicts the spirit of security, housing a row of dense trees representing sentinels with a reassuring message to the citizens of safe and secure borders.

Also drawing attention to the National Police Memorial dedicated to the men and women in uniform who were the first line of defence and response during calamities and crises, *Mann Ki Baat* stood witness to the twin memorials built in the national capital after seven long decades.

In addition to these memorials, the history of valour has been kept alive and vibrant by a slew of initiatives that have made their appearance on *Mann Ki Baat* from time to time. Especially on key commemorative days such as the Armed Forces Flag Day, the Police Commemoration Day and the annual days of the Indian Army, Indian Air Force and the Indian Navy.

Paying special attention to the Central Armed Police Forces and other law enforcement agencies, *Mann Ki Baat* marked Police Commemoration Day in October 2021, recounting how the number of women police personnel had doubled since 2014 with more than 2,15,000 daughters of India serving in uniform. With training underway in Specialized Jungle Warfare, female commandos who would be part of the Commando Battalion for Resolute Action (CoBRA) were sending a message of changing times across India. From airports and metro stations to government offices, brave women of Central Industrial Security Force are guarding sensitive installations. Prime Minister Modi noted the ripple effect of this enhanced presence of women security personnel on society. Observing how the policewomen had become role models for lakhs of girls across the country, he heralded what he termed as 'a new age of policing'.

Mann Ki Baat has also been a platform for the welfare of soldiers from its initial days, including the launches of the Gallantry Awards portal and the Sainik Kalyan Board portal. In order to counsel patience on the implementation of One Rank One Pension, PM Modi's personal appeal to the veterans to trust him drew upon a deep personal bond formed with soldiers and border forces over the years when he would spend Diwali with them. In 2014, it was at Siachen; in 2017, it was at Gurez; and at Nowshera in 2021. Discussing his annual tradition of spending

Diwali with men and women in uniform, PM Modi shared how the sacrifices, dedication and enthusiasm of the soldiers constantly occupied his thoughts and emotions. This connection fuelled his determination to dedicate Diwali celebrations to the security forces.

Launching a citizen initiative called Sandesh to Soldiers, *Mann Ki Baat* galvanized outreach between communities and the men and women in uniform. It became a medium for expressing sentiments by conveying strength and messages that proved to be a great morale booster. School and college students, villagers, the underprivileged, traders, shopkeepers, political leaders, sportspersons, people from the cine world—all lit a lamp for the country's jawans in a campaign to send greetings and salutations to the people who protect them.

> While we are celebrating Diwali in the comforts of our homes, some of these Jawans are deployed in the desert areas, others are guarding the towering Himalayan peaks, some are guarding our industrial establishments and some are maintaining security vigil at the airports. What great responsibilities they have on their shoulders! And so if we remember them also while we are in our festive mood, our remembrance gets a new vigour which gets imparted to them also and they feel a new strength. Just one message can enhance their capability and our country has shown it. I earnestly express my gratitude to all our countrymen and women for this gesture.[4]

---

[4]"PM's "Mann Ki Baat" Programme on All India Radio on 30 October 2016', *PMIndia*, 30 October 2016, https://tinyurl.com/bde7s8u6. Accessed on 7 April 2023.

Encompassing drawings, rangolis and cartoons as well as poems and couplets, Sandesh to a Soldier became a radio programme, apart from going viral on social media as a campaign. Hearfelt thanks were sent from a grateful nation to all those military personnel who stood as sentinels and fighters on every front. Motivated by a sense of patriotism, *Mann Ki Baat* turned the festival of lights into a celebration of the soldiers' service to the nation, whether they were from the Border Security Force (BSF), Central Reserve Police Force (CRPF), Indo Tibetan Border Police (ITBP), Assam Rifles, the navy, the army, the air force, the coast guard and all those who were valiantly facing great hardships in the line of duty.

ICONS THAT INSPIRE

It was not only tributes to soldiers in the line of duty that dominated the radio programme. *Mann Ki Baat* also stood out for the extensive tributes paid to two icons of India who have been a constant inspiration to the spirit of nationalism—Netaji Subhas Chandra Bose and Sardar Vallabhbhai Patel.

In the January 2019 episode, PM Modi recalled the contributions of the Indian National Army and the spirit of innovation, that went beyond merely a call to arms in fighting the British Empire:

> I have always considered radio as an effective means of connecting with people. Similarly, Netaji shared a deep bond with the medium of radio and he chose this very medium to converse with countrymen.
>
> In 1942, Subhas Babu established Azad Hind Radio and through it he used to communicate with soldiers of

the Indian National Army and other countrymen. Subhas Babu had a distinct style of opening a broadcast. In the opening he would begin with, 'This is Subhas Chandra Bose speaking to you over the Azad Hind Radio...'. These words instantly stirred up listeners with a rush of a new energy, a new fervour.

I am told this radio station also used to broadcast weekly news bulletins in English, Hindi, Tamil, Bangla, Marathi, Punjabi, Pashto and Urdu languages. In managing the affairs of this radio station, a resident of Gujarat M.R. Vyas ji played a vital role. Programmes broadcast over Azad Hind Radio were very popular amongst the populace. Their programmes were a major source of inspiration and strength to our freedom fighters.[5]

Mann Ki Baat has drawn inspiration from Sardar Vallabhbhai Patel over the past many years with the observance of the National Unity Day, celebration of the Statue of Unity, formulation of EBSB and the awards for national integration finding regular mention.

Sharing little known facets of Patel's role in unifying India, the PM detailed the events leading up to the integration of Lakshadweep islands.

Friends, all of us know that as India's first home minister, Sardar Patel undertook the colossal, historic task of integrating Princely states. Scrutinizing the minutest of events closely was his rare quality. On the one hand, he concentrated on Hyderabad, Junagarh and other States; on the other, he was watching far flung Lakshadweep intently.

---

[5]'PM's Mann Ki Baat Programme on All India Radio', *PMIndia*, 27 January 2019, https://tinyurl.com/3f4p52vj. Accessed on 9 April 2023.

Actually, when we refer to Sardar Patel's endeavour, his role in the unification of just a few notable States is discussed. He played a far more significant role, when it came to a small region such as Lakshadweep too. Lakshadweep is one of the most beautiful landscapes in India. Soon after Partition in 1947, our neighbour had cast an eye on Lakshadweep; a ship bearing their flag was sent there. When Sardar Patel was informed of this, he wasted no time in initiating stern action. He urged the Mudaliar brothers, Arcot Ramasamy Mudaliar and Arcot Lakshmanaswami Mudaliar to immediately undertake a mission with people of Travancore to Lakshadweep and take the lead in unfurling the Tricolour there. Following his orders, the Tricolour was promptly unfurled there and the nefarious dreams of the neighbour of annexing Lakshadweep were decimated within no time. After this incident, Sardar Patel asked the Mudaliar brothers to personally ensure all assistance for development of Lakshadweep.[6]

In his characteristic style, PM Modi revealed how Infantry Day came about due to the singular effort of the Iron Man of India based on anecdotes from India's pride, Field Marshal Manekshaw, also known as Sam Bahadur. In October 1947, Pakistani forces infiltrated Kashmir to capture territory. Explaining the historical context of how Indian forces landed in Kashmir and saved the valley from the clutches of aggression, listeners were regaled to stories of Field Marshal Manekshaw from when he was a colonel. In a meeting, Patel was irked by the delay in sending troops

[6]"PM's Address in the 5th Episode of "Mann Ki Baat 2.0'", *PMIndia*, 27 October 2019, https://tinyurl.com/4uvvxfnn. Accessed on 9 April 2023.

to Kashmir and, during the proceedings, gave Field Marshal Manekshaw a characteristic glance, reiterating that there should be no delay in army operations and that a solution should be sought swiftly. Immediately after that, the infantry troops flew to Kashmir, making history.

HEROES OUTSIDE THE FORCES

Taking the spirit of service to the nation beyond those in uniform, *Mann Ki Baat* has, over the years, celebrated the contributions of nurses, doctors, frontline workers, disaster response personnel and innumerable *karmayogis* (selfless workers) who have made an impact. The PM narrated the example of railway train ticket examiner (TTE), Bijaya Biswal, from Nagpur division, a gifted painter who, while working with the Indian Railways, has combined his passion and public purpose, by making interesting paintings related to railways. Similarly, he cited the example of Operation Malyudh, started by the entire team of government officials in Harda district, Madhya Pradesh, which gave a new direction to Swachh Bharat Abhiyan, and highlighted public officials going beyond the call of duty to gift toilets to sisters as a way of celebrating Raksha Bandhan.

The finest instance of karmayogis going beyond the call of duty was the effort to get hands-on with toilet pit cleaning, shared on *Mann Ki Baat* in February 2017. Prime Minister Modi highlighted the toilet pit emptying exercise that was carried out in Telangana on 17 and 18 February 2017 in six houses. It detailed the exemplary role played by officers who personally demonstrated how the used-up pits of twin-pit toilets can be emptied and then reused to dispel common stigmas attached with toilet cleaning.

He spoke of how the exercise showed results and inspired public officials and communities across India to clean toilet pits and set an example to all of India on making the country open defecation free (ODF).

An inspirational example of a karmyaogi was security personnel of the ITBP, Jawan Vikas Thakur, hailing from a small village in Sirmaur district of Himachal Pradesh. He handed a cheque of ₹57,000 to the head of the village panchayat with the request that ₹1,000 was given to each of the 57 households that had no toilets, so that 57 toilets could be constucted to ensure an ODF village.

NEW FORMS OF NATIONALISM

Nationalism as a creed for New India took many forms through *Mann Ki Baat,* from the Sankalp Parva in 2017 to the Har Ghar Tiranga campaign in 2022. Azadi Ka Amrit Mahotsav saw a creative melding of water conservation with patriotism to celebrate Mission Amrit Sarovar. It also saw rangolis, *lori*s (lullabys) and other creative means of expression manifesting into competitions to celebrate 75 years of Indian independence.

Govind Mohan, secretary to the Government of India in the Ministry of Culture, shared several interesting facts on the impact of *Mann Ki Baat* in taking nationalism to every household. Every call to action by PM Modi resulted in levels of participation far beyond what is typically expected of government sponsored initiatives. For example, Govind Mohan noted that the Har Ghar Tiranga campaign saw record sales of the national flag across India, with more than 25 crore flags sold nationwide, in what was a direct economic boost to weavers, small vendors and manufacturing enterprises. The rangoli, lori and patriotic song competitions, according to Mohan, saw more than 5,00,000 entries across 700 districts of India, with entries being sent in more than 20 languages.[7]

Inspiring young minds to envision India in 2047, when Indian independence from British colonialism marks its centenary, PM Modi's call to action saw more than 20 crore postcards mailed in by students across India. Mohan sees *Mann Ki Baat* as being singularly responsible for propelling messages on a national scale to stir creativity and inspire innovation, boosting the spirit of nationalism in an era of fragmented attention spans and ever-increasing digital distractions.

The spirit of patriotism amplified by *Mann Ki Baat* is best exemplified by its celebration of artistes across India and their love for traditional musical instruments and art forms reflecting unity in diversity.

A few days ago, 'Ustad Bismillah Khan Yuva Puraskar' were conferred. These awards were given away to emerging, talented artists in the field of music and performing arts. These, along with the rising popularity of the art and music world are also contributing in their enrichment. These also include artists who have breathed new life into those instruments, whose popularity was decreasing with time... Joydeep is persevering towards making the Sursingar popular once again. Similarly, the efforts of sister Uppalapu Nagamani ji are also very inspiring, who has been awarded in the category of Carnatic Instrumental on the Mandolin. On the other hand, Sangram Singh Suhas Bhandare ji has been

---

[7]In conversation with the author in March 2023.

awarded for War Varkari Kirtan. This list doesn't just pertain to music artistes—V Durga Devi ji has won this award for 'Karakattam', an ancient dance form. Another winner of the award, Raj Kumar Nayak ji, organized the Perini Odissi, which lasted for 101 days in 31 districts of Telangana. There is another award winner—Saikhom Surchandra Singh. He is known for his mastery in making Meitei Pung Instrument. This instrument has connections with Manipur. Pooran Singh is a Divyang Artist, who is popularizing various Music Forms such as Rajula—Malushahi, Nyuli, Hudka Bol, Jagar.[8]

Drones to interceptor missiles, anti-satellite tests to vaccine drives, no milestone was small and no achievement was insignificant for a celebration on *Mann Ki Baat*. It was the fruit of labour since October 2014 that the programme became a godsent platform for nationwide civic engagement during the Covid-19 lockdown and during the subsequent drives to vaccinate more than a hundred crore Indians.

My dear countrymen, today, our personnel from the medical field, frontline workers are all endeavouring 24x7 in service work. Similarly, other people of the society also are not lagging behind at this time. The country is once again united and fighting against Corona. These days, I see that someone is delivering medicines to families living in quarantine, someone is sending vegetables, milk, fruits etc. Someone is offering free ambulance services to patients. Even in such challenging times, in different corners of the country, voluntary organizations are coming forward

---

[8]"PM's Address in the 98th Episode of "Mann Ki Baat"", *PMIndia*, 26 February 2023, https://tinyurl.com/5n8rpnaa. Accessed on 9 April 2023.

and trying to do whatever they can to help others. This time, new awareness is also being seen in the villages. By strictly following the Covid rules, people are protecting their village from corona Covid-19, proper arrangements are also being made for those who are coming from outside. Many young people have also come forward in the cities, working together with the local residents, in order to prevent the rise of Corona cases in their area. Meaning, on the one hand, the country is working day and night for hospitals, ventilators and medicines and on the other hand, the countrymen are also fighting the challenge of Corona with a lot of heart. This resolve gives us so much strength, so much confidence. Whatever efforts are being made are of great service to the society. They strengthen the power of society.[9]

Mann Ki Baat's civic engagement in the service of the nation was put to test on a mass scale that none could have imagined or anticipated during the Covid-19 pandemic. Prime Minister Modi took to airwaves to thank the supply chain personnel who worked tirelessly to ensure oxygen supplies were made available across India; the lab technicians who, while at risk of high degree of exposure to the virus, were engaged in testing across India; among many other service providers. The rise in TV viewership during *Mann Ki Baat* broadcasts between 2020 and 2021 was a measure of how it came to play a central role in the service of the nation.

---

[9]"PM's Address in the 76th Episode of "Mann Ki Baat"", *PMIndia*, 25 April 2021, https://tinyurl.com/2s88vsbp. Accessed on 9 April 2023.

CHAPTER 3

REDISCOVERING THE ANCIENT, ASPIRING FOR THE MODERN

C limate change has come to dominate modern-day politics and political activism in much of the developed West. This has occurred even more so in the last few years, owing to increased efforts to influence policies across governments on issues ranging from sustainability to decarbonization. Climate politics in the West is largely identified with Left-leaning political movements that usually don the label of 'progressivism' as compared to Right-leaning 'conservatism'.

In India, the political templates of the West fall by the wayside, as PM Narendra Modi has defied the political stereotypes used in the West through a policy-level commitment to sustainability. To understand how he has broken through these stereotypes to champion sustainability, one has to take a journey through *Mann Ki Baat* over the years, in which he connects modern India's priorities with ancient India's principles. The PM considers the past to be a living guide that is constantly mentoring, informing, guiding and advising. *Mann Ki Baat* has, in many ways, brought ancient India's history alive to have a conversation with modern India on its path to development.

In the April 2018 episode, the PM touched upon a subject that has been dear to him for decades—water conservation. He took the opportunity to inform listeners about how water conservation has been a way of life in India for centuries. Recalling the due priority and importance given to each drop of water, he highlighted the many indigenous methods developed to conserve water. Talking about stone carvings in Tamil Nadu depicting irrigation systems, water conservation methods and drought management, he urged the listeners of *Mann Ki Baat* to visit historic sites in the state, such as Mannarkovil, Cheranmahadevi, Kovilpatti and Pudukkottai, to see these massive stone inscriptions. Drawing people's attention to *baori*s (stepwells), which have emerged as famous tourist spots, such as the UN Educational, Scientific and Cultural Organization (UNESCO) World Heritage site of Adalaj and Patan's Rani ki Vav in Gujarat, PM Modi called them temples of water conservation. Speaking about Chand Baori in Rajasthan, one of the biggest and the most beautiful stepwells of India, the PM drove home the point that water conservation has had an ethical and societal value in India from ancient times.

More than a year later, in November 2019, the programme veered back to this critical subject, during which the PM highlighted the manner in which ancient Indian culture celebrated rivers periodically, through festivals dedicated to 12 rivers across India.

My dear countrymen, Pushkaram, Pushkaraalu, Pushkaraha—have you ever heard these terms? Do you know what these are? Let me tell you. These are the different names by which festivals organized on 12 different rivers across the country are called. One river every year...that means it would recur on that particular river after 12 years... and this festival is held sequentially every year in 12 different rivers spread across the country... and it lasts for 12 long days. Just like the Kumbh festival, this too, encourages the concept of national unity. And echoes the philosophy of 'Ek Bharat Shreshtha Bharat' (One India Best India). [...] Pushkaram is a festival in which the greatness of the river, the glory of the river, the importance of the river in our lives... all these are brought forth naturally. Our forefathers put a lot of emphasis on nature, on environment, on water, on land, on forests. They understood the importance of rivers, and tried to inculcate a positive mindset towards rivers in the society. They constantly strove to conflate the river with the cultural stream, the stream of tradition, and with the society. And the interesting thing is that, not only did it bring the society closer to the rivers, it also brought people closer to each other. Last year, the Pushkaram was held on the Thamirabarani river in Tamil Nadu. This year it was held on the Brahmaputra River. Next year it will be held in Telangana, Andhra Pradesh and Karnataka on the Tungabhadra River.[1]

In April 2022, PM Modi once again invoked tradition and cultural values to speak about water conservation, highlighting its importance. He quoted ancient Indian scriptures to renew his appeal to citizens: *Paniyam paramam loke, jeevanam jeevanam*

---

[1]'PM's Address in the 6th Episode of "Mann Ki Baat 2.0"', *PMIndia*, 24 November 2019, https://tinyurl.com/3wz2b7f8. Accessed on 31 March 2023.

samritam (Water is most important for survival of life on our planet, all of life is encompassed in it).

Explaining the essence of the quote, he reiterated how water was the basis for all life on the Earth and the greatest resource for humanity. Recounting how water conservation was a persistent theme across great Indian epics, such as the Ramayana and the Mahabharata, PM Modi emphasized the need to connect water sources across India. Tracing India's water engineering heritage to the Indus–Sarasvati civilization, he spoke about how Harappan sites had interconnected systems of water sources. Paying special attention to indigenous wisdom in water conservation of several native tribes, the PM underscored how sustainable living was a universal ethic across ancient India's diverse cultures.

> Friends, every effort related to water is related to our tomorrow. It is the responsibility of the whole society. For this, different societies have made various efforts continuously for centuries. For example, Maldhari, a tribe of Rann of Kutch uses a method called Vridas for water conservation. Under this, small wells are built and trees and plants are planted nearby to protect it. Similarly, the Bhil tribe of Madhya Pradesh used their historical tradition Halma for water conservation. Under this tradition, the people of this tribe gather at one place to find a solution to the problems related to water. Due to the suggestions received from the Halma tradition, the water crisis in this area has reduced and the ground water level is also increasing.[2]

---

[2]"PM's Address in the 88th Episode of "Mann Ki Baat"", *PMIndia*, 24 April 2022, https://tinyurl.com/3a3mddyh. Accessed on 31 March 2023.

PAST INSPIRES THE PRESENT

The ancient Indian lessons on conservation and afforestation on *Mann Ki Baat* have inspired grassroots champions across India to share their voluntary efforts to combat climate change. An unusual instance of this is the inspirational manner in which Sonal Mhatre's wedding was hosted by her grandfather Khandu Maruti Mhatre, a farmer from Narayanpur village of Junner Taluka of Pune. Her grandfather came upon the idea of distributing saplings of the Kesar variety of mango, thus making her wedding an everlasting story of love for nature.

Speaking about this innovative effort, PM Modi recounted the 'Anushasan Parv', a chapter from the Mahabharata, that speaks of the belief that planting a tree begets an offspring in the form of that tree.

> There can be no doubt about this fact. He who donates a tree, that tree in return becomes a ladder to salvation just like children [sic]. Therefore, it is appropriate that parents desiring their well-being should plant tree and rear them like their own children.[3]

Drawing further examples from the Bhagavad Gita, PM Modi also highlighted how concern for the well-being of trees in the middle of the battlefield is a reminder of how our ancestors valued nature and conservation. Citing a quote from Shukracharya's treatise, he also drew the attention of the listeners to the medicinal value of every tree, plant and herb. Giving his own example from his days as the CM, PM Modi described how, at the Ambaji Temple

---

[3]"PM's "Mann ki Baat" Programme on All India Radio', *PMIndia*, 31 July 2016, https://tinyurl.com/mpmybxf9. Accessed on 31 March 2023.

in Gujarat, saplings were gifted as divine offerings to visiting devotees by a non-governmental organization (NGO), a practice that spread to other temples as well and encouraged afforestation and preservation of the green cover.

There are many instances of listeners echoing PM Modi and bringing to his attention the manner in which our ancient heritage can inspire solutions to modern-day problems of conservation. Manish Mahapatra from Puducherry urged PM Modi to inform the nation about how India's native tribes and their ancient traditions are great examples of coexistence with nature for sustainable development. PM Modi's reply, shared on *Mann Ki Baat*, is a retelling of India's native history from the vantage point of modern-day sustainability.

> Manishji, I appreciate you for bringing this subject among the listeners of Mann Ki Baat. This is one subject that inspires us to look into our dignified past and our ancient traditions. Today, the whole world and specially the western countries are discussing about environment protection and are trying to find new ways to adopt a balanced life style. Our country is also facing this problem. But, for its solution we only have to look inwards, to look into our glorious past and our rich traditions and have especially to understand the lifestyle of our tribal communities. To live in consonance and close coordination with the nature has been an integral part of our tribal communities. Our tribal brethren worship trees and plants and flowers like gods and goddesses. The Bhil tribes of Central India and [especially] those in Madhya Pradesh and Chhattisgarh worship Peepal and Arjun trees religiously. The Bishnoi community in the desert land of Rajasthan has shown us a way of environment protection. Specially, in the

context of serving trees, they prefer laying down their lives but cannot tolerate any harm to a single tree. Mishmi tribes of Arunachal Pradesh claim their relationship with tigers. They even treat them like their brothers and sisters. In Nagaland as well, tigers are seen as the forest guardians. People of Warli Community in Maharashtra consider tigers as their guests and for them the presence of tigers is a good omen indicating prosperity. There is a belief among the Kol community in Central India that their fortune is directly connected with the tigers and they firmly believe that if the tigers do not get food, the villagers will have to face hunger. The Gond tribe in Central [India] stops fishing in some parts of Kaithan river during the breeding season. They consider this area as a fish reserve and they get plentiful of healthy fishes because of this belief of theirs. Tribal communities make their dwelling units from natural material, which are strong as well as eco-friendly. In the isolated regions of the Nilgiri plateau in South India, a small wanderer community Toda make their [sic] settlements using locally available material only.[4]

Beyond sustainable solutions for climate change from our heritage, the PM also used ancient symbols of prosperity to popularize modern-day economic initiatives. In one of the early episodes of *Mann Ki Baat*, Modi introduced an initiative for monetizing gold, timed with the Indian festival of Dhanteras that is known for its tradition of gold buying. With the introduction of gold coins bearing the Ashok Chakra, the eternal wheel symbolizing dharma from the Mauryan era, he demonstrated how cues from

---

[4]"PM's Mann Ki Baat Programme on All India Radio", *PMIndia*, 28 October 2018, https://tinyurl.com/35bm9kws. Accessed on 31 March 2023.

the ancient past were key to motivating and inspiring behavioural change in modern India.

Interestingly, the PM applies ancient history as a compass to navigate modern life's many challenges seamlessly across subjects—from water conservation to overcoming examination anxieties around mathematics—even as he continues to engage his listeners. Elaborating on how the idea of zero was conceived by ancient Indian mathematicians, he drew upon India's rich mathematical heritage to boost confidence in young minds to tackle upcoming examinations. The PM's championing of mathematics through *Mann Ki Baat* stands in stark contrast with recent developments in the United States (US) where mathematics in school curricula has taken a backseat across several school districts.[5] Two Sanskrit quotes drawn from ancient Indian texts helped bring home the point on how ancient India valued math skills.

यत किंचित वस्तु तत सर्वं, गणितेन बिना नहि!‌[6]

(There is no objective measure of any item or substance without mathematics.)

एकं दशं शतं चैव, सहस्रम् अयुतं तथा।
लक्षं च नियुतं चैव, कोटिः अर्बुदम् एव च।।
वृन्दं खर्वो निखर्व च, शंखः पह्मः च सागरः।
अन्त्यं मध्यं परार्धः च, दश वृद्ध्या यथा क्रमम्।।[7]

(एकं = 1 = 10^0; दशं = 10 = 10^1; शतं=100=10^2; सहस्रम् = 1,000 = 10^3; अयुतं = 10,000 = 10^4; लक्षं = 100,000 = 10^5; नियुतं = 1,000,000 = 10^6;

[5]Aleksey, Allyson, 'Parents Challenge SF School District's Math Policies in Court', *San Francisco Examiner*, 21 March 2023, https://tinyurl.com/yc7cc2ey. Accessed on 19 April 2023.

[6]"PM's Address in the 88th Episode of "Mann Ki Baat"', *PMIndia*, 24 April 2022, https://tinyurl.com/4ad3w43t. Accessed on 5 April 2023.

[7]Ibid.

कोटि: = 10,000,000 = 10^7; दशकोटि: = 100,000,000 = 10^8; अर्बुदम = 1,000,000,000 = 10^9; वृन्दं = 10,000,000,000 = 10^{10}; खर्वो = 100,000,000,000 = 10^{11}; निखर्व = 1,000,000,000,000 = 10^{12}
Such are the powers of 10 in sequence.)

Underscoring how math bridges the ancient with the modern, PM Modi spoke about a painting gifted to him by the CEO of Intel, in which an Indian method of arithmetic computation and measurement was depicted through Vamana, one of the 10 avatars of Lord Vishnu, in which he appears as a brahmin of dwarfish stature to restore dharma or the natural order on the Earth. From extolling the contributions of Pingala, an ancient Indian poet-mathematician to celebrating modern Indian mathematicians like Srinivasa Ramanujan, PM Modi's focus on math has been on motivating young minds to overcome their fears and anxieties and celebrating uniquely Indian ways of thinking about math. In fact, the efforts of Gaurav Tekriwal, educator and founder-president of the Vedic Maths Forum India, at popularizing Indian methods of arithmetic under the banner of Vedic math received a tremendous boost after his conversation with PM Modi on *Mann Ki Baat*. Through the Samagra Shiksha Abhiyan, conducted by the Government of India, Tekriwal's Vedic math has reached out to students and teachers alike across multiple states, to simplify arithmetic and to popularize uniquely Indian ways of thinking about math (while drawing inspiration from ancient methods and techniques).[8]

The roving eye of PM Modi's *Mann Ki Baat* over the past nine years has constantly been on the lookout for ancient icons to kindle scientific curiosity within young Indian minds. December

---

[8]'Vedic Math Impacts 10 Lakh Students under Samagra Shiksha', *ANI*, 27 January 2022, https://tinyurl.com/4r8467fc. Accessed on 10 April 2023.

2019 was one such occasion, where young listeners were not only regaled with tales of ancient astronomers and mathematicians, such as Aryabhatta and Bhaskara, but were also introduced to Madhava of Sangamagrama, who is credited with having developed mathematical techniques of calculus more than a century prior to Isaac Newton. Exhorting the youth towards a culture of star gazing and studying the night sky, Modi shared a lesser-known Gujarati work on the ancient science of navigation.

> The night sky was not merely something that whetted the curiosity. It was an important source for mathematicians and scientists. A few years ago, I had unveiled a book called *Pre-modern Kutchi Navigation Techniques and Voyages*. This book, in a way, is the diary of Maalam. Maalam was a navigator and whatever he experienced professionally, he recorded it in his diary. Even in the modern age, the very same 'Maalam's volume' exists as a collection of ancient Gujarati manuscripts. It describes ancient navigation technology, and that 'Maalam's volume' repeatedly references, the sky, the stars, the speed of the stars, and clearly describes how the direction is determined in sea voyages with the help of stars; it is stars that navigate us towards our destination.[9]

BEYOND MYTHS: BREAKING MOULDS

Prime Minister Narendra Modi's invocation of the ancient to negotiate the modern has gone beyond dispelling myths and fears to breaking stereotypes and clearing misconceptions. Ancient

---

[9]"PM's Address in the 7th Episode of "Mann Ki Baat 2.0"", *PMIndia*, 29 December 2019, https://tinyurl.com/2ehydkpr. Accessed on 31 March 2023.

India's naval history was the focus of the November 2017 episode of *Mann Ki Baat*. Tracing the heritage of Indian seafaring from the Chola dynasty to Chhatrapati Shivaji, PM Modi spoke at length on the strategic and economic significance of sea and fresh water routes while also highlighting the role of women seafarers who played a crucial role in the Chola Navy.

Ancient wisdom and modern science came together again in February 2018 when the programme focussed on the emerging trends in artificial intelligence (AI) and the immense potential it held for India's future development. Recalling the words of Sri Aurobindo, Modi emphasized the ancient Indian ethic of interrogating abstract ideas in the pursuit of knowledge.

I am fortunate today to be in Auroville, the land, the karmabhoomi of Maharshi Arvind. As a revolutionary, he challenged British rule, fought against them and questioned subjugation. Thus, as a great sage, he questioned every facet of life. Extracting answers, he showed the right path to humanity. The relentless quest to ask questions for knowing the truth is very important. And this is the very essence[—]the real inspiration behind scientific inventions and discoveries. Never rest till every 'why', 'what' [and] 'how' are answered.[10]

Prime Minister Modi's melding of the ancient with the modern has consistently focussed on breaking gender stereotypes in India, as reflected in the episode that observed the death anniversary of Kalpana Chawla, the first Indian-origin woman astronaut who lost her life during the Space Shuttle Columbia disaster in

---

[10]'PM's Mann Ki Baat Programme on All India Radio', *PMIndia*, 25 February 2018, https://tinyurl.com/36jzebmt. Accessed on 31 March 2023.

February 2003. Ever since her first space flight, Kalpana has been an inspirational figure in India, motivating girls across the country to dream big and aspire to reach the stars. Recalling Kalpana's life story and the lessons it held for women across India, PM Modi dwelt at length on *nari shakti* (power of women). Quoting the Skanda Purana, he reminded his listeners how ancient India valued and worshipped the girl child.

> Today, we talk about 'Beti Bachao, Beti Padhao' (save the girl child, educate her). But centuries ago, it has been mentioned in our ancient texts, in the Skanda Purana:
>
> दशपुत्र–समाकन्या, दशपुत्रान् प्रवर्धयन
> यत फलम् लभते मर्त्यः, तत् लभ्यम् कन्यकैकया ।।
>
> This means, a daughter is the equivalent of ten sons. The '*Punya*' [virtuous merit] that you earn through ten sons amounts to the same earned through just one daughter.[11]

'Shakti', as a metaphor for the status and role women enjoyed in ancient India, draws from a long tradition of *vidushi*s or women scholars.

From composing Vedic verses to expounding on philosophy, the scholarship of Lopamudra, Gargi and Maitreyi is as significantly inspirational to modern Indian young women as Kalpana Chawla's achievements. Threading ancient and medieval times alongside modern India, PM Modi's reference to iconic women and their life stories spans multiple eras and traverses the diversity across India—from Akka Mahadevi to Meerabai, Ahilyabai Holkar to Rani Lakshmibai.

---

[11]'PM's Mann Ki Baat Programme on All India Radio', *PMIndia*, 28 January 2018, https://tinyurl.com/4vyk76za. Accessed on 31 March 2023.

Developing this theme of seeking ancient Indian metaphors in taking the pursuit of gender equity in modern India further, the PM, in September 2019, initiated the 'Bharat ki Lakshmi' campaign to celebrate daughters. Alluding to the goddess of prosperity ahead of the autumn festival season in India, he called on citizens to honour and celebrate the accomplishments and achievements of Indian women, drawing attention to their perseverance, hard work, diligence, courage and enterprise.

This elicited an overwhelming response across India, with several stories of grit, determination and societal impact of daughters of modern India being shared on social media, and subsequently, in the October 2019 episode of *Mann Ki Baat*. From Major Khushbu Kanwar, the daughter of a bus conductor, who has led an all-women contingent of Assam Rifles, to the life story of a 92-year-old woman who has been offering free drinking water to passengers at Gwalior Railway Station, Bharat ki Lakshmi became a nationwide movement on celebrating women. This modern-day celebration based on the ancient Indian cultural symbol of 'lakshmi' also brought attention of the nation to unsung heroines and their lesser-known works.

> [The] well-known 17th century poetess Sanchi Honnamma has penned a poem in Kannada that embodies the same thought, the same words pertaining to every Lakshmi of India that we referred to. One feels the foundation of the idea was laid in the 17th century itself. You will notice the beauty of word, sentiment and thought in this poem in Kannada:
>
> (*Penninda permegondanu himavantanu.*
> *Penninda broohu perchidanu*
> *Penninda janakaraayanu jasuvalendanu*)

Which means, Himwant, Lord Mount, attained fame on account of daughter Parvati, Rishi Brighu on account of his daughter Lakshmi and King Janak because of daughter Sita. Our daughters are our pride... their prodigious virtuosity cradles our social fabric, ensuring its bright future.[12]

India's ancient heritage, while being a constant companion all through *Mann Ki Baat*, neither blinded PM Modi from drawing attention to present-day challenges, nor detracted from modern science when it came to motivating mass-scale behavioural change to deal with the societal challenges confronting India. Covid-19 was perhaps the biggest test of effectiveness of PM Modi's melding of the past with the present, to chart a course for the future. While consistently advising citizens across India to practice yoga and seek succour from traditional Indian healing techniques, such as Ayurveda, *Mann Ki Baat* was upfront in taking on vaccine hesitancy. Prime Minister Modi's simultaneous advocacy of modern medical science alongside ancient methods of healing and well-being ensured India administered well over 200 crore vaccine doses, surpassing entire nations and continents. With the Indian economy fully open even as neighbouring China struggled with lockdowns, *Mann Ki Baat* demonstrated that seeking inspiration from the ancient to find harmony with the modern was not an abstract idea, but a practical way of life that can deliver large-scale results by inspiring mass behavioural change.

---

[12]'PM's Address in the 5th Episode of "Mann Ki Baat 2.0"', *PMIndia*, 27 October 2019, https://tinyurl.com/4uvvxfnn. Accessed on 31 March 2023.

CHAPTER 4

ATITHI DEVO BHAVA REDEFINED

India, the land of myriad languages, cultures and cuisines, has long attracted travellers from distant shores. Domestic tourism, however, has largely been defined by religious pilgrimages and spiritual retreats. *Mann Ki Baat*, in many ways, has sought to magnify the thrust for domestic tourism by inspiring and motivating the aspirational middle class to explore the wonders of India and appreciate its beauty and diversity. In the process, it has provided much-needed boost to local economies.

Prime Minister Modi has often talked about the importance of tourism in India, encouraging his listeners to travel and explore their own country. The importance of the promotion of cultural and historical heritage of India; the need to preserve significant sites; and making them accessible to tourists was highlighted by the popular digital campaign #IncredibleIndia, which went viral. In tandem with government efforts to boost the infrastructure of many tourist spots in India through the development of efficient transport, accommodation and other facilities, *Mann Ki Baat* has been a champion for local businesses and enterprising individuals making a living out of tourism. A fine example of these efforts is the launch of MV (motor vessel) Ganga Vilas, the world's longest river cruise, by the PM in January 2023. As it sails from Varanasi (PM Modi's constituency) to Dibrugarh in Assam via Bangladesh, it connects preservation and conservation of the environment with economic development and cross-cultural tourism.

Taking his appeal for tourism beyond culture, history and religion, PM Modi's championing of wildlife and natural tourism received a tremendous boost with Discovery Channel's Bear Grylls exploring the Jim Corbett National Park with PM Modi in 2019 on *Man vs Wild.*

> After the broadcast of this show, a large number of people have been discussing [...] Jim Corbett National Park. You must also visit sites associated with nature and wildlife and animals. As I have said before, and I emphasize, [...] you must visit the *north-east* in your lifetime. What a glorious abundance of nature exists there. You will be left wonderstruck! Your horizon will expand. On 15th August, I urged all of you from the ramparts of the Red Fort to visit at least 15 places within a span of the next 3 years, 15 places within India and for 100% tourism, visit these 15 sites! Witness and observe. Do take the family and spend some time there.[1]

The PM soon followed up his appeal with the *Mann Ki Baat* episode of September 2019 returning to the subject of tourism to mark World Tourism Day. Drawing the attention of his listeners

---

[1] 'PM's Address in 3rd Episode of "Mann Ki Baat 2.0', *PMIndia*, 25 August 2019, https://tinyurl.com/yckp5ycj. Accessed on 31 March 2023.

to the improvement of India's ranking in the International Travel and Tourism Competitiveness Index, PM Modi linked his tourism push with his other flagship mission of cleanliness. Crediting the Swachh Bharat Abhiyan for the significant jump in India's ranking from 65 to 34 on this index over a period of five years, Modi gave a first glimpse of his forward thinking on *Mann Ki Baat*, with the upcoming seventy-fifth anniversary of Indian Independence. Fast-forward to 2022 and the programme is championing iconic places linked to India's history and its struggle for Independence. This is yet another demonstration of how *Mann Ki Baat* has sustained key themes over a nine-year span, constantly revisiting ideas and innovating on the emotive appeal to engage citizens. The pinnacle of this effort was the Statue of Unity in Kevadia, Gujarat, to celebrate independent India's geographical architect Sardar Vallabhbhai Patel. Prime Minister Modi took to airwaves to share how international tourism has impacted the little-known tribal hamlet of Kevadia a year after the statue was dedicated to the nation. Sharing statistics on how more than 26 lakh tourists visited Kevadia over the 12 months since the unveiling of the Statue of Unity, PM Modi underscored the impact on the local economy through the many convenience services generating local employment and villagers providing homestays to visiting tourists.

> Friends, for our nation and the constituent states, as well as for the tourism industry, this 'Statue of Unity' can be a subject of research. We are all witness to […] how within a year a place developed as a world-famous tourism destination. People arrive there from [within] the country and abroad. And one after the other, ancillary services like transport, lodging, guides and eco-friendly services are getting

inducted by themselves. A large economy is developing and people are generating facilities as per the requirement of the tourists. The government is also playing its role. Friends, which Indian will not be imbued with pride for the fact that recently, Time magazine has included the 'Statue of Unity' in its list of 100 important tourist destinations around the world. Of course, I hope, that all of you will devote some of your precious time to visit the 'Statue of Unity'. But my appeal is, that every Indian who takes out time to travel must visit at least 15 Tourist Destinations of India with family and experience a night stay at whichever place you go to; this still remains my appeal.[2]

In October 2020, while recalling Sardar Patel's efforts to unify India politically after independence, the PM dwelt at length on how spirituality and pilgrim centres have played a culturally unifying role over the centuries. Recalling the pan-India mission of Adi Shankaracharya, a Hindu saint who traversed the length and breadth of the subcontinent more than 1,500 years ago, PM Modi described the unifying effect of the four *matha*s or monasteries established by Shankaracharya in all four directions of India—Badrikashram in the north, Puri in the east, Sringeri in the south and Dwarka in the west. He explained to the listeners how the chain of *jyotirlingas* (sacred stone formations to worship Lord Shiva and Shakti Peethas, dedicated to the worship of the many forms of Goddess Shakti) have knit India into a cultural unit over the centuries. Through this, PM Modi sought to emphasize the central role of faith in motivating pilgrims and unifying Indian

---

[2]'PM's Address in the 5th Episode of "Mann Ki Baat 2.0"', *PMIndia*, 27 October 2019, https://tinyurl.com/4uvvxfnn. Accessed on 31 March 2023.

society. He underscored the intrinsic link between spirituality and India's rivers as follows:

> The various rivers in our country are invoked before each ritual, ranging from the Indus located in the far north to the Kaveri, the lifeline of South India. Often people in our country say or chant while bathing with a hallowed belief, the mantra of unity:
>
> *Gange Che Yamune Chaive Godavari Saraswati.*
> *Narmade Sindhu Kaveri Jale asminn Sannidhim Kuru*
>
> [In this water imbue the holiness of rivers Ganga, Yamuna, Godavari, Saraswati, Narmada, Indus and Cauvery.]
>
> Similarly, the holy sites of Sikhs include 'Nanded Sahib' and 'Patna Sahib' Gurdwaras. Our Sikh Gurus too have enriched the spirit of unity through their lives and noble deeds.[3]

THE LIGHTHOUSE CASTS A SPOTLIGHT

The impact of *Mann Ki Baat*'s championing of India's iconic locations and tourism destinations was perceived early both on social media and in publications. In 2015, *HuffPost* documented the social media impact of a digital photo album of Incredible India initiated by the PM through *Mann Ki Baat*, where he called upon his listeners to share pictures of their travels.[4] With several

---

[3]'PM's Address in the 17th Episode of "Mann Ki Baat 2.0"', *PMIndia*, 25 October 2020, https://tinyurl.com/3jt8b6k2. Accessed on 5 April 2023.

[4]Nayar, Aashmita, 'Modi Is Marketing Incredible India on Social Media and It's a Pretty Sight', *HuffPost*, 3 June 2015, https://tinyurl.com/46mjmwuf. Accessed on 23 March 2023.

lakh likes and shares within a few days, the social media initiative went viral, showcasing everything from the little-known Belum Caves in Kurnool and Prinsep Ghat in Kolkata to the world-famous Golden Temple in Amritsar. From sunrise in Arunachal Pradesh to sunset in Kanyakumari, the initiative spurred from the studio of *Mann Ki Baat* continues to draw attention to tourism destinations across India to this date. The pan-India impact of this championing of tourism is evident from the fact that the Orchha Fort in Madhya Pradesh, which was highlighted by Modi in his June 2015 episode, became a shooting location seven years later, for the Tamil historical blockbuster *Ponniyin Selvan*.[5] Menal Waterfall, which was also highlighted in the same episode in 2015, continues to be rated as one of the best places to visit in Rajasthan by several online travel websites.

Drawing a deep connection between iconic landmarks of India (from medieval and ancient times) and conservation and preservation, *Mann Ki Baat* has made tourism as much about the economy as about the environment and, more specifically, about water conservation. Highlighting the engineering genius underlying these iconic landmarks, PM Modi brought to the fore the importance of science and technology for preservation and conservation.

> All of us have seen houses and buildings being constructed of bricks and stones but can you imagine that about twelve hundred years ago, a giant mountain, which was a single-stone mountain, was [given] the shape of an elegant, huge and a unique temple. [This] may be difficult to imagine,

---

[5]Janani K., 'Trisha Shares BTS Pic and Video from Ponniyin Selvan Shoot in Madhya Pradesh. Seen Yet?', *India Today*, 19 August 2021, https://tinyurl.com/22cvbuev. Accessed on 10 April 2023.

but this happened and that temple is Kailasnatha Mandir in Ellora, Maharashtra. Would you believe if someone tells you that about a thousand years ago, an over sixty metres tall pillar of granite was built and another granite rock weighing about 80 tonnes was placed over its top. But, Brihadeeswara temple of Thanjavur in Tamil Nadu is the place where this unbelievable combination of engineering and architecture can be seen. Anybody will feel overawed on seeing Rani Ki Vav of the 11th Century in Patan in Gujarat. Our land has been an engineering laboratory. There have been several engineers in India who made the unimaginable possible and presented such marvels of engineering before the world. In this lineage of great engineers, we were blessed with a diamond whose work is still a source of wonder for all. He was Bharat Ratna Dr. M. Visvesvaraya. Lakhs of farmers and common people continue to benefit from the Krishna Raja Sagara Dam built by him.[6]

From the Vivekananda Rock Memorial in Kanyakumari at the southern tip of the Indian peninsula to the Rann of Kutch on the western frontiers of India, *Mann Ki Baat* has played the role of a lighthouse of sorts, casting the spotlight on some of the lesser-known destinations. It was, thus, no surprise that Guruprasad of Chennai, who has popularized *Mann Ki Baat* in the Tamil language through his volunteer efforts, felt inspired to explore the lighthouses in Chennai and Mahabalipuram and share his experience with *Mann Ki Baat* listeners. Recounting the impact of the PM's words, he says, 'Recently, I visited the temple mentioned

---

[6]'PM's "Mann ki Baat" Programme on All India Radio', *PMIndia*, 26 August 2018, https://tinyurl.com/a855wsvm. Accessed on 31 March 2023.

by Modi ji in his *Mann Ki Baat* episode of January 2023 and saw the inscriptions mentioned by him. I was told by local authorities that the temple had now become a tourist attraction, with many visitors coming to see the inscription.'[7]

Speaking of maritime tourism, the March 2021 episode of *Mann Ki Baat* brought the listeners' attention to India's oldest lighthouse in Mahabalipuram and the Shore Temple built during the Pallava era by King Mahendravarman I.[8] He referred to 71 lighthouses across India and called for their economic development as tourism hubs with the addition of museums, amphitheatres, open air theatres, cafeterias, children's parks, eco-friendly cottages and landscaping. The programme took its listeners to Jhinjhuwada in the Surendranagar district of Gujarat to an inland lighthouse more than a hundred kilometers away from the western coast of the Arabian Sea to reiterate the importance of conservation in the face of climate change.

SYNCRETIC THREAD BETWEEN TOURISM AND INCLUSIVITY

Restoration of landmarks associated with iconic personalities has been a hallmark of PM Modi's tenure over the past nine years. Most prominent among these are the Panchteerth, or the five blessed places associated with Dr B.R. Ambedkar— his *janmabhoomi* (birthplace) in Mhow, his home in London, the *deeksha bhoomi* (place of of initiation [into Buddhism]) in

---

[7]In conversation with the author in March 2023.
[8]Kumar, Sharanya, 'Is This 7th-Century Temple India's Oldest Lighthouse?', *Traveller*, 6 December 2022, https://tinyurl.com/4cpf5tdy. Accessed on 10 April 2023.

Nagpur, his *mahaparinirvan sthal* (place of death) in Delhi and the *chaitya bhoomi* (final resting place) in Mumbai. *Mann Ki Baat* has witnessed how PM Modi has melded social inclusion and tourism by drawing inspiration from these landmarks associated with the life journey of Ambedkar. Viewing these landmarks as an inspiration for the Dalit community and the underprivileged, PM Modi, through his dialogue, dedicated the landmarks to those Indians who, despits adversities in their personal lives, have strived for success. Weaving a syncretic thread across tourism and inclusivity, *Mann Ki Baat* reached out to the expanding diaspora of Indian students overseas on how Ambedkar's memorial could emerge as a modern-day pilgrim centre where the youth could draw lessons from his life.

Mann Ki Baat has been a magnet for India's diaspora, drawing them back to the land of their ancestors to rediscover its ancient ethos and modern practices through tourism and pilgrimages. Paying tribute to one such listener from the diaspora, PM Modi underscored the modern-day significance of ancient observances to tourism.

What I am going to tell you now will make you really happy... you will be proud of our heritage. Shriman Kanchan Banerjee, who lives in America, has drawn my attention to one such campaign related to the preservation of heritage. I congratulate him. Friends, this month, Tribeni Kumbh Mahotshav was organized in Bansberia of Hooghly district in West Bengal. More than eight lakh devotees participated in it... But do you know why it is so special? It is special, since this practice has been revived after 700 years. Although this tradition is thousands of years old, but unfortunately this festival which used to take place in Tribeni, Bengal, was stopped 700 years ago. It should have been started after Independence, but that too could not happen. Two years ago, the festival has been started again by the local people and through 'Tribeni Kumbho Porichalona Shomiti'. I congratulate all the people associated with its organization. You are not only keeping alive a tradition, but are also protecting the cultural heritage of India.[9]

There is perhaps no greater brand ambassador for Indian travel and tourism than PM Narendra Modi. Through *Mann Ki Baat*, he has drawn global attention to India's age-old ethic of *Athithi Devo Bhava* (a guest is akin to God), welcoming visitors to India. His championing of iconic places and historical sites has resulted in not merely a cultural shift, but also in increased economic activity across these destinations.

---

[9]"PM's Address in the 98th Episode of "Mann Ki Baat"", *PMIndia*, 26 February 2023, https://tinyurl.com/5n8rpnaa. Accessed on 31 March 2023.

CHAPTER 5

IMBUING POSITIVITY: THE GLASS IS HALF FULL

Utsaaho balwaanarya, Naastyutsaahaatparam balam |
Sotsaahasya cha lokeshu na kinchidapi durlabham ||

[A] man full of enthusiasm is very strong since there is nothing more powerful than zest. Nothing is impossible for a man having positivity and zeal.[1]

If there is one word that can describe *Mann Ki Baat* in its entirety, it would be 'positivity'. It is often expected of a democracy, and a developing one at that, to focus its attention on deprivation, misery, conflict and strife. Almost all of what passes for progressive activism in modern-day democracies has focussed on the advocacy of doom and the pursuit of gloom. It is this negative and nihilistic form of community activism—that had spread like

---

[1]'PM's "Mann Ki Baat" Programme on All India Radio', *PMIndia*, 31 December 2017, https://tinyurl.com/2p8kbuvn. Accessed on 31 March 2023.

a termite infestation into the frame of Indian democracy—that PM Modi has sought to arrest with *Mann Ki Baat*. Through his relentless focus on positivity, PM Modi has exuded a missionary zeal to pursue much-needed societal change rather than allow the status-quo to persist. He has upheld collective action over conflict while narrating stories of selflessness over strife. With India's youth as his focus, PM Modi's *Mann Ki Baat* has been a constant endeavour to prevent the future leaders of India from falling into the twin negative traps of pessimism and cynicism.

IDEA OF A NEW INDIA

Through *Mann Ki Baat*, PM Modi's interaction with the youth has encompassed three primary areas: addressing youth concerns and promoting sports; fostering entrepreneurship; and encouraging innovation through science, technology and start-ups. His continuous motivation of the youth over the past nine years has been sustained by narrating India's development journey and highlighting the many milestones crossed along the way. A key theme in these years has been celebrating the present while setting the pace for the future. Underlying this vision of development that can be realized by the efforts and commitment of the present-day youth has been PM Modi's conception of New India.

Back in March 2017, *Mann Ki Baat* revealed the thought process behind the idea of New India. It was neither a product of government initiatives nor the outcome of government spending, but was meant to be a citizen's initiative led by the community itself. Recognizing that such a transformed India would require restoration of the fabric of trust across the society, PM Modi made a strong case for the primacy of rules and fair play.

If every citizen resolves to obey traffic rules, if every citizen resolves that he will discharge his duties honestly, if every citizen resolves that he will not use petrol or diesel one day in a week—these are not very big things. But these will contribute to the realisation of the dream of this country, this 'New India', that is being nurtured by 125 crore countrymen, and this realisation will be achieved before their eyes. In essence, every citizen must discharge his civic duties and responsibilities. This in itself would be a good beginning to the New India.[2]

Following up on this idea of New India, in July 2017, *Mann Ki Baat* spelled out a resolution that would commit individuals, communities, civil society and the entire nation towards achieving the necessary change. As India was set to mark 70 years of Independence then, the programme took due note of the efforts taken to rid the country of its ills and the hard work put in to increase employment, alleviate poverty as well as development. Most importantly, recognizing how expectations have risen, PM Modi mentioned how the years 1942 to 1947 were decisive years for attainment of Independence through a strong resolve. He foresaw a similar need in the period from 2017 to 2022.

We should celebrate 15th August 2017 as the Sankalp Parva or the Day of Resolve, and in 2022 marking 75 years of Freedom, we will certainly transform that resolve into 'Siddhi' or attainment.[3]

[2]'PM's "Mann ki Baat" Programme on All India Radio', *PMIndia*, 26 March 2017, https://tinyurl.com/ydwh4ewu. Accessed on 31 March 2023.
[3]'PM's "Mann ki Baat" Programme on All India Radio', *PMIndia*, 30 July 2017, https://tinyurl.com/muxh8u77. Accessed on 31 March 2023.

Little did he know that three years later, the entire world would be plunged into a once-in-a-hundred-years crisis posed by the Covid-19 pandemic. It is to the credit of his leadership and foresight that his mantra of 2017 showed the way to brave the pandemic. Two years later, in 2022, India emerged with an even stronger resolve to build itself anew through self-reliance. His call to action in 2017 was for individuals and communities to come together, persevere and work relentlessly with utmost strength towards the making of New India.

> Every Indian, social organisations, local self-government institutions, schools, colleges, various organizations—all should take one resolve or the other for a New India. A resolve that we will positively fulfil in the next five years. Youth organisations, student organisations, NGOs, etc. can organise group discussions, to bring forth new ideas. Where do we want to reach as a nation? What can be my contribution for this as an individual? Let us come together and make this a Festival of Resolve.[4]

SALUTING 'NEW INDIA YOUTH'

The mass movement for New India acquired a concrete mission statement of sorts when PM Modi called on first-time voters to look at their vote as much more than just participating in elections. Exhorting the youth to play a defining role in determining and deciding the course of the nation in the twenty-first century, *Mann Ki Baat* challenged them to imagine themselves as the makers of a twenty-first-century India, infused with energy and resolve. Prime

---

[4]Ibid.

Minister Modi described them as 'New India Youth' and that New India epitomized their aspirations, enthusiasm and energy. He also expressed his belief that the dream of New India would be realized through the skill and fortitude of India's energetic youth. Envisioning a new India of equal opportunity and aspirations, he articulated the need of the hour: to build a mass movement for making a 'magnificent, glorious 21st century India; a mass movement of development, a mass movement to build a capable and strong India'. [5]

Fast-forward to 2022, and one gets to witness this five-year movement expand into a 25-year commitment to transform India, with *Mann Ki Baat* setting a roadmap for a developed India by the year 2047.

> Friends, the biggest message that emerges from all these events being organized in the Azadi Ka Amrit Mahotsav is that all of us countrymen should follow our duty with full devotion. Only then will we be able to fulfill the dream of those countless freedom fighters... and to build the India of their dreams. That is why this Amrit Kaal of our next 25 years is Kartavyakaal, a period of duty for every countryman. To liberate the country, our brave fighters had given us this responsibility, and we have to fulfill it fully. [6]

[5] 'PM's "Mann Ki Baat" Programme on All India Radio', *PMIndia*, 31 December 2017, https://tinyurl.com/369prsnp. Accessed on 31 March 2023.
[6] 'PM's Address in the 91st Episode of "Mann Ki Baat"', *PMIndia*, 31 July 2022, https://tinyurl.com/24vk3rhm. Accessed on 31 March 2023.

SPORTING ACHIEVEMENTS: A NATIONAL CELEBRATION

Saluting the spirit of the young achievers and exhorting the importance of their hard work and determination, *Mann Ki Baat* has focussed on their success stories (across sports, science and technology as well as other innumerable fields), with even the smallest of selfless contributions, in the remotest of villages gaining national attention. This effort to celebrate and recognize the achievements of young Indians has made *Mann Ki Baat* a platform for recognition of excellence, inspiring the youth to believe in themselves with a can-do attitude. The unrelenting focus on positivity has ensured that this initiation to inspire and motivate the youth goes viral, with more and more examples of positive change being highlighted through the radio programme.

Most popular instances of these are from the world of sports, with the impact of various interventions beginning to show results across global competitions. Underscoring the importance of a strong resolve and a deep, boundless fervour for excellence, PM Modi imparted a poignant lesson to his young listeners on overcoming hurdles by relating the success stories of sportspersons. From Asian Games to Commonwealth Games; World Championships to the Olympics; from individual feats to team victories—every sporting accomplishment was a cause for national celebration.

Over the last nine years, across more than 90 episodes, there is hardly an episode without a mention of sports. In these examples, PM Modi has focussed on more than 20 sporting events—from team sports like hockey and cricket to traditional Indian sports like Mallakhamb to Kalaripayattu—at the global and local levels, with Khelo India Youth Games getting special attention. Prime Minister Modi has also praised more than 50 sportspersons across these episodes.

Alongside icons like Neeraj Chopra, P.V. Sindhu, Mithali Raj and Virat Kohli, who have been celebrated on *Mann Ki Baat*, emerging champions from humble backgrounds also became role models to inspire and motivate the youth on the radio programme.

[The] media discussed extensively about the 16-year-old Rajani. You too must have read it. Rajani has won a gold medal at the Junior Women's Boxing Championship. The moment Rajani won the medal she rushed to a nearby milk stall & drank a glass of milk. After that, she wrapped a cloth around the medal & kept it in a bag. You must be wondering why Rajani did that! She did it in honour of her father Jasmer Singh ji who sells lassi at a stall in Panipat. According to Rajani, her father has sacrificed a lot, undergone hardships to help her reach where she is. Early every morning, Jasmer Singh used to leave for work before Rajani and her siblings woke up. When Rajani approached her father, expressing her wish to learn boxing, he encouraged her, arranging for whatever possible resources that he could. Rajani had to start her training in boxing with old gloves, since those days, the family was not too well financially. Despite so many hurdles, Rajani did not lose heart and went ahead with her training in boxing. She has won a medal in Serbia too. My best wishes and blessings to Rajani. I also congratulate her parents Jasmer Singh ji and Usha Rani Ji for supporting & encouraging Rajani.[7]

Delving deeper into the personal life stories of sportspersons beyond fame and laurels, PM Modi has inspired hope in the face

[7]'PM's Mann Ki Baat Programme on All India Radio', *PMIndia*, 30 December 2018, https://tinyurl.com/58pu77tc. Accessed on 31 March 2023.

of adversity. Stories like those of Narayan Thakur (the disabled orphan who used to make a living cleaning public transport buses and serving food at roadside eateries before he went on to win a gold medal for India in 2018 Asian Para Games) and Thangjam Tababi Devi (the Youth Olympics silver medallist judoka who is the daughter of a labourer and fish-seller) motivated the listeners to not let hardships dampen their zest and enthusiasm to excel.[8] Through the inspirational story of 20-year-old Vedangi Kulkarni from Pune, who became the fastest Asian to traverse the globe riding a bicycle, PM Modi highlighted how passion can motivate exemplary achievements, even if it meant riding around 300 km every day for 159 days.[9]

It is, however, from Khelo India that the most compelling life stories have emerged on *Mann Ki Baat*, setting the stage to nurture future champions who will go on to compete globally and make India proud. Khelo India, which means 'sporting India', has been focussed on giving a national platform to talented sportspersons from every corner of India, irrespective of their backgrounds.

> Only when the local ecosystem of our sports will be strong i.e. only when our base will be strong, then only our youth will be able to perform their best in the country and across the world. When the player performs his best at the local

---

[8]Aranha, Jovita, 'Grew Up In Orphanage, Cleaned Buses & Won Gold For India: This Boy Defines True Grit!', *The Better India*, 24 October 2018, https://tinyurl.com/35bz732j. Accessed on 10 April 2023; Sharma, Nitin, 'Youth Olympics 2018: Fish Vendor Mother, Labourer Father and Village Wait for Judo Silver Winner Tababi Devi', *The Indian Express*, 9 October 2018, https://tinyurl.com/bwcb4ddh. Accessed on 10 April 2023.

[9]'India's Vedangi Kulkarni Cycles the Globe in 159 Days, Becomes Fastest Asian to Achieve the Feat', *India Today*, 24 December 2018, https://tinyurl.com/4re4as5b. Accessed on 10 April 2023.

level, only then, he also shines globally.

[...] I was reading that young Akash Gorkha who won a silver medal in boxing had his father, Ramesh Ji working as a watchman in a complex in Pune. They live in a parking shed with their family. The captain of Maharashtra Under-21 Women's Kabaddi team, Sonali Helvi is from Satara. She lost her father at a very young age, and her brother and mother encouraged the talent and skills of Sonali.

It is often seen that girls are not encouraged much to participate in sports such as Kabaddi. In spite of the hurdles, Sonali not only chose Kabaddi but excelled in this discipline. 10-year-old Abhinav Shaw hailing from Asansol is the youngest gold medallist in the Khelo India Games. A farmer's daughter, Akshaya Basavani Kamat, from Karnataka won a gold medal in weightlifting. She credited her victory to her father, a farmer in Belgaum.[10]

Mann Ki Baat has not only celebrated their talent but also put the spotlight on the humble backgrounds of these budding sportspersons and on the personal challenges and sacrifices made by their families in helping them pursue their passion.

Father of Adil Altaf from Srinagar, who won the gold in 70 km cycling, does tailoring work, but, has left no stone unturned to fulfill his son's dreams. Today Adil has brought pride to his father and the entire Jammu-Kashmir. Gold winner L. Dhanush's father is a carpenter in Chennai. Sangli's daughter Kajol Sargar's father works as a tea vendor. Kajol would help her father and practice weight lifting as well.

---

[10]'PM's Mann Ki Baat Programme on All India Radio', *PMIndia*, 27 January 2019, https://tinyurl.com/3f4p52vj. Accessed on 31 March 2023.

This hard work of hers and her family paid off and Kajol has won a lot of accolades in weight lifting. Tanu of Rohtak has performed a similar kind of miracle. Tanu's father Rajbir Singh is a school bus driver in Rohtak. By winning the gold medal in wrestling, Tanu has realized her own, her family's and her father's dream.[11]

In his quest to inspire the Indian youth, PM Modi made a rare departure from sporting events and went beyond Indian shores by drawing attention to a viral video on social media of Daniil Medvedev, a Russian tennis player, who reflected on winning and losing after an intense final for the men's singles title at the US Open in 2019.

These are moments that go way beyond winning and losing, where victory and defeat cease to matter. It is the life that is a victory…. This has been beautifully articulated in our scriptures. The wisdom of our ancestors is truly praiseworthy. Our ancient texts observe:

विद्या विनय उपेता हरति
न चेतांसि कस्य मनुजस्य
मणि कांचन संयोगः
जनयति लोकस्य लोचन आनन्दम

means, when ability and humility amalgamate in a person, whose heart will he not be able to win over? As a matter of fact, this young player has won the hearts of people across the globe.[12]

---

[11]'PM's Address in the 90th Episode of "Mann Ki Baat"', *PMIndia*, 26 June 2022, https://tinyurl.com/3m2e62sy. Accessed on 31 March 2023.
[12]'PM's Address in 4th Episode of "Mann Ki Baat 2.0"', *PMIndia*, 29 September

CHAMPION CHANGE-MAKERS

To express PM Modi's belief in having a continuous dialogue with the youth, *Mann Ki Baat* was as much a medium for conversation as it was for listening and learning. Viewing the youth as a storehouse of ideas and a powerhouse of energy, focus and innovation and sharing their efforts, *Mann Ki Baat* has emerged as an invaluable instrument in the creation of New India. Acknowledging the inquisitive nature of the youth, PM Modi, in the fiftieth episode of *Mann Ki Baat* in November 2018, shared insights into their mindset. He recognized their respect for time, desire for innovation and eagerness to achieve goals rapidly. He saw India's youth as dreamers with grand ambitions. Further dwelling on this theme in August 2021, he spoke about the spirit of New India, showcasing the youth's ability to multitask; dream big; courageously attempt the unprecedented; and aspire to bring societal change through social enterprises and various ventures. Bringing their stories to life, PM Modi has gone beyond sports to highlight young change-makers and innovators.

When we cast a keen glance at the young generation, we notice a sweeping change there. The mind of the youth has undergone a transformation. And today's young minds, shunning obsolete, age old methods and patterns, want to do something new altogether; something different. Today's young mind does not want to tread readymade beaten paths; it wants to carve out newer paths. It wants to step on unknown territory. New destinations, new goals as well, new roads, new aspirations as well! And once a young

2019, https://tinyurl.com/5cm4wnus. Accessed on 31 March 2023.

person decides in the mind, no stone is left unturned in the pursuit... persevering day and night. We see how, some time ago, when India opened her Space Sector... within no time the young generation lapped up the opportunity. And to avail of its benefits, college students and young people working in universities and the private sector enthusiastically came forward. And I firmly believe that in the coming days, a large number of satellites would be of those developed by our youth, our students, our colleges, our universities, students working in labs.

Similarly, wherever you see... go to any family... however well to do, however educated the family might be... if you speak to a young person in the family, she or he, moving away from family traditions, express the wish to do a start up or join a start up... excitedly willing to take a risk. Today, the startup culture is expanding even to smaller cities and I am seeing it as an indication of a bright future. Just a few days ago, toys in our country were being discussed. Within no time, when this caught the attention of our youth, they too resolutely decided to work towards positioning Indian toys in the world with a distinct identity. And they are trying out ever new experiments. The world is a huge market for toys... a market of Rs. 6 to 7 lakh crores. Today, India's share is miniscule. But, how to craft toys, what diversity to be lent to toys, what technology to be used, how toys should be, compatible with child psychology... these are points where the youth of the country is applying minds to... wishing to contribute something.[13]

---

[13]'PM's Address in the 80th Episode of "Mann Ki Baat"', *PMIndia*, 29 August 2021, https://tinyurl.com/pkkrrp6u. Accessed on 31 March 2023.

One such change-maker, Ripu Daman Bevli, who has popularized 'plogging' in the spirit of Fit India and Swachh Bharat, recalls his experience:

> I run an initiative called Kuda Mukt Bharat or litter-free India. In 2016, I started plogging—picking up litter while jogging. In 2019, I received a phone call from PM Narendra Modi and, for about 15 minutes, he listened to me to understand what plogging was. At the intersection of Fit India and Swachh Bharat, plogging today has become a national movement thanks to the impact of *Mann Ki Baat*. Several million Indians have taken up plogging, contributing to the mission of a clean and plastics free India.[14]

UPSTARTS: THE WORLD OF START-UPS

Prime Minister Narendra Modi's grassroots experiences from his formative years taught him that the word 'innovation' was not merely about high-end technology and the digital world of apps and gadgets, but also referred to everyday out-of-the-box thinking even by labourers and rural workers to make a difference to their communities and society at large.

It is, therefore, no surprise that, *Mann Ki Baat*, with the support of investors from all over the country and abroad, has recorded a culture shift in India. This shift from job security and starting salary mattering the most to young college graduates a few years ago, to start-ups and risk-taking through ventures now is perceptible. Prime Minister Modi insists that this is a turning point in India's growth story, where people are not only dreaming

---

[14]As told to Doordarshan in March 2023.

of becoming job seekers but also of becoming job creators.

Listeners have been introduced to some of these job creators through *Mann Ki Baat*. We have learnt of Anurag Agarwal and Sidhi Karnani's foray into organic farming in Sikkim; Vishwas Dwivedi's digitalized tiffin transportation to blue collar workers; Dignesh Pathak's innovation around animal feeds; and Manoj Gillda Nikhil's start-up that solves challenges around agri-storage.[15]

The impact of *Mann Ki Baat*'s championing of Indian start-ups and Modi's celebration of the energy, enthusiasm and determination of India's youth has been most visible in the months after the pandemic. The massive investment into start-ups across India, including in small towns, has seen a major milestone being reached by India in mid-2021—a record of 70 Unicorns (start-ups whose valuation is at least a $1 billion, or more than ₹7,000 crores). Interestingly, a year later, in May 2022, the number of Unicorns in the country reached 100. The total valuation of these Unicorns was more than $330 billion or ₹25 lakh crore. With a diverse set of Unicorns operating in many fields like e-commerce, fin-tech, ed-tech and bio-tech, the world of Indian start-ups is beginning to reflect the spirit of New India, that PM Modi had first envisaged back in 2017.

The evolution of a complete support system in the country for start-ups, including mentors, means that India will see a new flight of progress in the start-up world.

---

[15]Chauhan, Ashish, '"Mann ki Baat" Praise for IIM-A Alumni's Sikkim Firm', *The Times of India*, 1 February 2016, https://tinyurl.com/yk6dvf6j. Accessed on 10 April 2023; 'शहर के युवक का जिक्र, मोदी बोले–ऐसे बनो तो बात बने', *Bhaskar*, 2016, https://tinyurl.com/5n7xwmvp. Accessed on 10 April 2023; 'English Rendering of the Text of Prime Minister's "Mann ki Baat" on All India Radio, 31st January 2016', *PMIndia*, 31 January 2016, https://tinyurl.com/4aunwdwm. Accessed on 10 April 2023.

Friends, behind this success of the country, the youth-power of the land, the talent and the government here, all are putting in efforts together... everyone is contributing. But another thing that is important in the world of Start-Ups is, right mentoring, that is, right guidance. A good mentor can take a start-up to new heights... can guide the founders in every way toward the right decision. I am proud that there are many such mentors in India who have dedicated themselves to promote Start-ups.

Sridhar Vembu ji has recently received the Padma Award. He himself is a successful entrepreneur, but now he has also taken up upon himself the task of grooming other entrepreneurs. Shridhar ji has started his work from a rural area. He is encouraging the rural youth to do something in this area, staying in the village itself. We also have people like Madan Padaki who had created a platform named 1BRIDGE in 2014 to promote rural entrepreneurs. Today, 1BRIDGE is present in more than 75 districts of southern and eastern India. More than 9000 rural entrepreneurs associated with it are providing their services to rural consumers. Meera Shenoy ji is also one such example. She is doing remarkable work in the field of market linked skills training for rural, tribal and disabled youth. [16]

Mann Ki Baat also traces the path from passion to innovation to popularity, as highlighted by the story of Sai Praneeth Burah, a blogger who has come to be known as the Weatherman of Andhra Pradesh. He begins each day by studying all numerical

---

[16]"PM's Address in the 89th Episode of "Mann Ki Baat"", *PMIndia*, 29 May 2022, https://tinyurl.com/p2fuxceh. Accessed on 31 March 2023.

weather models, decoding the satellite images for almost two to three hours and scanning radar images from his mobile whenever he gets time. He prepares a weather update and posts real-time updates on social media to alert people on weather conditions. Sai Praneeth has emerged as a social media innovator and a role model, and received praise from PM Modi in the July 2021 episode of *Mann Ki Baat* for his unique efforts towards giving weather updates through innovative use of social media. As an early user of social media from his student days, his weather updates on Facebook attracted more than 25,000 followers. Fast-forward to 2022, Sai Praneeth's YouTube channel disseminating critical weather updates in his native language Telugu, during the recent cyclone Mandous, attracted an average of 2,00,000 views per video. Even mainstream media, such as the *Times of India*, quoted him. He was featured by *The Hans India*, and *The Week* listed him as one of the independent weathermen in India in its January 2023 edition. Sai Praneeth's social media adventure is helping the farmers of Andhra Pradesh brave the vagaries of weather during the monsoon season.[17]

Imbuing positivity with a perspective that always views the glass as half full, PM Modi's *Mann Ki Baat* has done more than any national effort in recent memory to celebrate India's present, while creating hope for a better future. As an advocate for dreaming big, PM Modi, through *Mann Ki Baat*, has played the role of a coach and mentor to the youth of India and inspired them to shape India's future.

---

[17]Nandakumar, Prathima, 'What Makes India's Independent Weathermen "Click"', *The Week*, 8 January 2023, https://tinyurl.com/bdz6jk3d. Accessed on 24 March 2023.

CHAPTER 6

RISING, YET ROOTED

The finest sportspersons achieve their excellence only when shaped and moulded by the best of coaches. The role of the coach goes beyond honing skills and techniques and into motivating and challenging to aspire for greater heights and bigger records to continuously excel. Prime Minister Modi, through *Mann Ki Baat*, has played exactly this role in encouraging not merely India's research labs and deep-tech start-ups but every budding scientist, aspiring engineer and starry-eyed entrepreneur. His method has been quite unique. While he has celebrated satellite launches and scientific breakthroughs, he has also focussed on drawing inspiration from deep within. He has been able to strike a balance between spirituality and science through yoga, Ayurveda and all that is innately Indian, to enrich both the soul and the mind.

At a time when developed societies in the West have been struggling to sustain their scientific edge with declining student interest in math and science skills, PM Modi focussed his message on the centrality of science in India's technological advancement, through children. *Mann Ki Baat* has raised awareness on the need to develop a scientific temperament by explaining to families why it is important to impress the role science plays in everyday life upon children. Taking the example of poor vision that has become commonplace with excessive use of digital devices, PM Modi has sought to convey how the science underlying optical vision and electronics could be explained to children.

> How does a calculator work, how does a remote-control work, what are sensors? Along with this, are such scientific elements also discussed in the house? Maybe we can easily explain these things behind the everyday functioning of the household, what is the inherent science behind a phenomenon.[1]

CSR 2.0

Evoking natural curiosity and taking the conversation beyond the virtual world to the skies above, *Mann Ki Baat* called on parents and teachers to participate in stargazing with children. Prime Minister Modi underscored the importance of knowledge about the night sky, stars and constellations by engaging his younger audiences in a conversation on the unlikeliest of subjects for a political leader—physics and astronomy. He drew the attention of his listeners to many smartphone apps that can aid in exploring the night skies, locating stars and planets and identifying constellations and galaxies. He has, thus, enabled his young listeners to fix their sights on the horizons of scientific advancement even as he called for

---

[1]'PM's Address in the 86th Episode of "Mann Ki Baat"', *PMIndia*, 27 February 2022, https://tinyurl.com/49atpuby. Accessed on 31 March 2023.

deep tech start-ups to take root in India. Viewing scientific abilities as crucial to nation-building, *Mann Ki Baat* advanced the notion of a collective scientific responsibility (CSR) towards the country.

It is this notion of CSR that saw India take tremendous strides in the space sector and weather the challenges posed by the pandemic. Behind both the space success and pandemic efforts was an early-stage thought process, which becomes clear from *Mann Ki Baat* episodes of 2014–15. Speaking on the commendable research being done in India by an outstanding generation of scientists, PM Modi's mind was already focussed on how to take scientific research to the common man; how to translate the academic theories to practical innovations; and how to connect 'laboratories to land', as he often remarked.[2]

A year later, in February 2016, as India joined a global network of laboratories making news on the discovery of gravitational waves, *Mann Ki Baat* had much to say about science in India and Indian scientists. Drawing examples from the life stories of Thomas Alva Edison and India's mathematical genius Srinivasa Ramanujan, PM Modi delivered an important message on the virtue of patience and how failure is inherent to harvesting success. He recognized the innately dynamic nature of scientific discovery and shared a profound mantra of how 'curiosity was the mother of science'.[3] His emphasis on the need to adopt scientific thinking and to innovate continuously with his call for 'Make in India Science and Technology Driven Innovations' was evidence of PM Modi's notion of collective responsibility towards the country.

[2]'Lab-to-Land: Modi's Slogan to Increase Agri Production', *Business Standard*, 29 July 2014, https://tinyurl.com/3s535bmu. Accessed on 31 March 2023.
[3]'English Rendering of the Text of Prime Minister's "Mann ki Baat" on All India Radio', *PMIndia*, 28 February 2016, https://tinyurl.com/3wd5hr3y. Accessed on 31 March 2023.

You must have heard recently there has been a major and important discovery in the world of science. Scientists have laboured hard, generations of them have persevered, and after nearly 100 years they have gained a huge success. Gravitational Wave has been brought to light with the efforts of our scientists. This is a success for science which was very difficult to achieve. It is going to be of use for the whole of humankind. But being Indians, we should all feel happy that in the entire process of this discovery, the sons of our country, our worthy Indian scientists, were also a part of it. I would like to extend my hearty congratulations to all those scientists.[4]

Foreseeing a technology-driven future and understanding the need to dynamically respond to rapid advancements, PM Modi recognized that technology can no longer be shackled. To maintain relevance, governments and leaders must stay in step with the swiftly evolving world of technology, ensuring that research and innovation become cornerstones for keeping abreast of global trends. Using strong words, in July 2016, the PM cautioned how, in the absence of research and innovation, technology will stagnate, 'just as still water stagnates and even stinks'.[5] He expressed concern over the use of old technology without recourse to research and innovation, and warned of the risks posed by the rapid pace of obsolescence.

With the mantra of 'let us aim to innovate', PM Modi's notion of collective responsibility started to take shape in the form of the Atal Innovation Mission. Envisioning a country-wide ecosystem

---

[4]Ibid.

[5]'PM's "Mann ki Baat" Programme on All India Radio', *PMIndia*, 31 July 2016, https://tinyurl.com/mpmybxf9. Accessed on 31 March 2023.

through this mission, he called for forging a vibrant chain of innovation, experimentation and entrepreneurship, which would also enhance the possibilities of new employment generation. In order to foster a culture of innovation, he sought to to set up 'Atal Tinkering Labs' in schools, with ₹10 lakh in seed funding and further ₹10 lakh for maintenance over five years. From schools to start-ups, people have been encouraged to not merely tinker with technology but to also incubate ideas that could turn into solutions for real world problems with the setting up of Atal Incubation Centres (envisaged with a funding of up to ₹10 crore). Threading it all together with the idea of identifying grand challenges facing society that could be solved by science and technology, under the umbrella of Atal Grand Challenges, PM Modi revealed that the government would play its role in collective responsibility towards science and technology by rewarding innovative solutions to the diverse problems facing the nation.

> I am happy that people have evinced interest in these things. When we spoke of Tinkering Labs, about 13 thousand schools applied and when we talked of Incubation Centres, over four thousand academic and non-academic institutions came forward. I firmly believe that the real tribute to Abdul Kalam ji will consist of harnessing research and innovation for developing technology to find solutions to problems we face in day to day life, and ridding us of the difficulties we face to make things easier for us all. The more the new generation devotes itself to this task, the greater will be their contribution with immense significance for the modern India of the 21st century. [6]

---

[6]Ibid.

EYES ON THE STARS, FEET ON THE GROUND

Space as the next frontier has perhaps dominated the discourse of *Mann Ki Baat* over the years. The early emphasis on space received tremendous boost, with the Mars Mission capturing global attention on how 'frugal' innovations from India had ensured an entry to the global club that included a handful of nations. To PM Modi, every space launch was a reason to reinforce the importance of technology in everyday life, and a reason to remind and motivate his young listeners to make science a part of their DNA.

> The sky and stars have always enthralled children. Our Space Program provides an impetus to the children to think big and reach across those boundaries, which were considered impossible till today. It is a vision to inspire the children to discover new stars, while gazing at them![7]

The impact of linking curiosity about space to fire the imagination of young minds was visible as early as June 2016 with students of the College of Engineering, Pune, designing an academic satellite. Giving them competition was SATHYABAMASAT, designed by the students of Sathyabama University of Chennai. Both of these were part of multiple satellites launched simultaneously by the Indian Space Research Organisation (ISRO), which was fast developing a niche for low-cost space technologies and opening up its services to other countries.

By February 2017, the ISRO's capacity for multi-satellite launches had crossed the hundred-satellite threshold, with the

---

[7]'PM's Mann Ki Baat Programme on All India Radio', *PMIndia*, 27 January 2019, https://tinyurl.com/3f4p52vj. Accessed on 31 March 2023.

US, Israel, Kazakhstan, Netherlands, Switzerland and United Arab Emirates (UAE) availing the ISRO's commercial launch services. From highlighting the role of women scientists in the development of Cartosat-2D to the impact of South Asia Satellite on developmental priorities of the neighbourhood, *Mann Ki Baat* proved to be a consistent champion of the Indian space sector, keeping up the morale of the scientists while inspiring and motivating aspiring space innovators. The students' enthusiasm over space technology development in India continued to grow with recent innovations like Kalamstat and sounding rockets as well as the use of NavIC by fishermen, (an indigenously developed navigation system in January 2019), which was celebrated by *Mann Ki Baat*. Dwelling on the developmental impact of space technology, PM Modi, in the January 2019 episode of the programme, shared critical statistics on how space technology was contributing to the economic development, apart from improving the delivery and accountability of government services. For instance, the Housing for All Mission involves geotagging of about 40 lakh homes spread over 23 states. Along with this scheme, about 3 crore 5 lakh properties under the Mahatma Gandhi National Rural Employment Guarantee Act (MNREGA) 2005 were also tagged.

In spite of the mixed success of India's Moon mission, Chandrayaan-2, PM Modi made very important points about the risks associated with experimentation and the need to never give up hope despite obstacles and stumbling blocks. He counted faith and fearlessness as the two great lessons from the mission, which was entirely the product of Indian innovation and scientific endeavour. Drawing life lessons from the mission for his young listeners, PM Modi spoke about how temporary setbacks are a fact of life and that the strength to overcome these setbacks, resides inwards.

Six months later, PM Modi took to airwaves to look ahead from Chandrayaan-2 to rally the nation towards a solar mission in the future. From envisioning Gaganyaan to putting a human in space and motivating students to develop a deeper understanding of space technology through the ISRO's Yuvika programme by 2022, PM Modi's tryst with India's space programme culminated in the ultimate goal of spawning space start-ups in India. With a progressive policy in place to open up the sector to private enterprises, in his nine years as the PM of India, he has enabled the tremendous expansion of the ISRO's commercial capabilities as well as, the beginning of an Indian space industry with the launch of IN-SPACe and the emergence of space start-ups like Agnikul, Skyroot and Dhruva Space.

As a sign of how inclusive India's efforts at opening up the space sector were, *Mann Ki Baat* turned the spotlight on Tanveer Ahmed's work at Digantara on mapping space junk and Neha Satak's work at Astrome on developing low-cost flat antennas. With 750 school students working on 75 experimental satellites, the story of Tanvi Patel from Mehsana in Gujarat epitomized the spirit of *Mann Ki Baat*, inspiring girls to dream big and aim for the stars. Prime Minister Modi summed up the societal and national impact of space reforms most eloquently in June 2022:

> Friends, these are the same youth, in whose mind the image of the space sector was like a secret mission a few years ago, but, the country undertook space reforms, and the same youth are now launching their own satellites. When

the youth of the country is ready to touch the sky, how can our country be left behind?[8]

Similar reforms in the drone sector saw India's innovative start-ups imagine uniquely Indian applications for drones. Giving an example of how apples are transported through drones in Kinnaur, Himachal Pradesh, when there is heavy snowfall, PM Modi spoke about how thinking and achieving big was fuelling an innovation renaissance in India. Pointing ahead to a Techade—a decade of Indian technology and innovation gaining global prominence—he recounted the transformation of IITs from academic institutions to incubation hubs for the next generation of start-ups focussed on 5G, AI and healthcare innovations crucial to India's development.

SILICON TO SOUL

This innovation focus, however, remained firmly rooted in the native soil and also aimed for the open skies. Modernizing traditional Indian sciences, such as Ayurveda, and championing AYUSH (Ayurveda, yoga and naturopathy, unani, siddha, sowa rigpra and homoeopathy) start-ups like Kapiva, NirogStreet, Atreya Innovations, Ixoreal and Cureveda, PM Modi underscored the importance of healthy, mindful living in an era of silicon-powered distractions. Where satellites, rockets and drones fired the imagination of *Mann Ki Baat*'s young listeners, PM Modi grounded their spirits with yoga and Ayurveda to chart a path to holistic wellness and living in harmony with the self and nature. Aiming to replicate the success of start-ups in other domains

---

[8]"PM's Address in the 90th Episode of "Mann Ki Baat"", *PMIndia*, 26 June 2022, https://tinyurl.com/3m2e62sy. Accessed on 31 March 2023.

by leveraging the spirit of innovation and entrepreneurship, the AYUSH Start-Up Challenge, promoted through *Mann Ki Baat*, had a significant impact. It led to the Global AYUSH Investment and Innovation Summit, which attracted investment proposals worth thousands of crores. It was clear that PM Modi's AYUSH push had its roots in yoga when, in June 2015, a little-known government department responsible for traditional Indian sciences was tasked with the monumental responsibility of organizing the International Day of Yoga.

> Science and Technology are value neutral. They don't possess any value in themselves. Any machine will work the way we want it to. It entirely depends on us what task we want it to perform. Here human objectives assume significance; the use of science for the sole purpose of human welfare, with the endeavour to assist human lives touch the greatest heights.[9]

Mann Ki Baat's soulful contemplation on the power of yoga to kindle inner strength is best appreciated from the life story of Anvi from Surat. Anvi was afflicted with Down syndrome since birth and had been battling serious heart disease since childhood. She even had to undergo open-heart surgery at barely three months of age. She could barely stand but was inspired to learn yoga as a means to reduce her dependence on caregivers. Anvi's yoga journey through trials and tribulations culminated in her being able to participate in international competitions and winning medals. The amazing changes in Anvi's life and persona through yoga resulted in greater self-confidence and reduced dependence on medications.

---

[9]"PM's Mann Ki Baat Programme on All India Radio", *PMIndia*, 25 February 2018, https://tinyurl.com/36jzebmt. Accessed on 31 March 2023.

I think Anvi is a good case study for those who want to test the power of yoga. Such scientists should come forward with studies based on Anvi's success and introduce the world to the power of yoga. Any such research could be of great help to children afflicted with Down's syndrome around the world.[10]

The PM's championing of yoga and Ayurveda has gone beyond touting its antiquity to bringing it much-needed scientific validation and rigour of research. The PM has highlighted the importance of evidence-based research to take AYUSH to the next level while remaining true to its spirit of scientific enquiry by drawing attention to efforts currently underway in mainstream medicine to integrate the best of yoga and Ayurveda.

The Centre for Integrative Medicine and Research (CIMR) established within the All India Institute of Medical Sciences (AIIMS) in New Delhi has been a pioneer in this effort, with over 20 peer-reviewed papers on the integration of yoga and AYUSH with modern medical methods and practices published in international journals. This achievement found a mention in *Mann Ki Baat* in December 2022. Reflecting on its impact on the CIMR's efforts, Dr Gautam Sharma, a cardiologist at AIIMS, said, 'The episode generated tremendous interest in the media about the scientific rigour associated with the effort to integrate yoga with modern medicine.'[11] He also believes that the PM's vision to establish the true potential of yoga resonates with the mandate of the CIMR. He adds, 'This has sparked a further interest in the

---

[10] 'PM's Address in the 93rd Episode of "Mann Ki Baat"', *PMIndia*, 25 September 2022, https://tinyurl.com/y7tn5ym3. Accessed on 31 March 2023.

[11] Basu, Soma, 'Integrated Medicine System to Alter Future of Disease Management', *The Hindu*, 9 March 2023, https://tinyurl.com/4ueu8tfn. Accessed on 27 March 2023.

medical fraternity, and has inspired us to work harder and more intensively in this area.'[12]

As celebrating individuals and institutes plays a stellar role in taking yoga to the people, PM Modi introduced the global recipients of the Prime Minister's award for outstanding contribution towards promotion and development of yoga to his listeners. He mentioned: Italy's Antonietta Rozzi (who has started Sarv Yoga International and popularized yoga throughout Europe); Bihar School of Yoga, Munger; Swami Rajarshi Muni of Life Mission, Gujarat; and Japan Yoga Niketan. The programme highlighted how yoga as a way of life was reaching out to citizens in India and also people across the globe.

Stressing on the potential of yoga as an effective physical and mental wellness tool, PM Modi waded into a subject that is little discussed in India. Discussing the taboos surrounding depression and the need to have open conversations within families regarding mental health, *Mann Ki Baat* raised much needed awareness on the subject.

> I want to tell my countrymen, that depression is not incurable. There is a need to create a psychologically conducive environment to begin with. The first mantra is the expression of depression instead of its suppression. Share openly what you are going through, with your colleagues, friends, parents, brothers, and teachers.[13]

A fitting tribute to the deep and uniquely Indian tradition of connecting science and spirituality was paid by PM Modi when

---

[12]In conversation with the author in March 2023.

[13]'PM's "Mann ki Baat" Programme on All India Radio', *PMIndia*, 26 March 2017, https://tinyurl.com/ydwh4ewu. Accessed on 31 March 2023.

he recalled the foundation of the Indian Institute of Science (IISc), India's premier science research institution in Bengaluru. It is popularly known as the child of the confluence of thoughts between two visionaries: India's foremost entrepreneur Jamsetji Tata and India's greatest ambassador of spirituality Swami Vivekananda.

> Jamsetji Tata was a true visionary, who not only foresaw India's future, but also duly laid strong foundations. He knew very well that making India a hub of science, technology and industry was imperative for her future. It was his vision that culminated in the establishment of the Tata Institute of Science, which we know as Indian Institute of Science today. On a voyage to America, Jamsetji Tata met Swami Vivekananda on the ship, and an important topic of their discussion was the outreach and spread of science & technology in India. [...] this very discussion led to the founding of the Indian Institute of Science[14]

From yoga to mental health, Ayurveda to science, *Mann Ki Baat* is as much a platform for science and technology as a guidebook for wellness and self-improvement. Calling attention to India's legacy of scientific enquiry, PM Modi's dialogue has gone where no public discourse by a PM had ever gone before.

---

[14]"PM's Mann Ki Baat Programme on All India Radio', *PMIndia*, 24 February 2019, https://tinyurl.com/5n7xjj24. Accessed on 31 March 2023.

CHAPTER 7

A METAPHOR FOR INDIA'S DIVERSITY

Acknowledging the interconnectedness between India's farmers and its abundant biodiversity; expansive coastlines and forests; and towering snow-capped mountains, there is a noticeable shift towards embracing natural farming methods. Showing the way is Spiti, nestled in the state of Himachal Pradesh.

Revealing little-known facets of this tribal area, PM Modi, on *Mann Ki Baat*, informed the nation of this symbiosis and the way it can lead to optimal utilization of local resources while ensuring food security (through high farm yields) even in challenging hilly terrains. Spiti is a tribal area and pea plucking is a common farm activity there, which is quite laborious and difficult on hill farms. The women of the village gather as a community and pluck peas from each other's fields together. Farmers who rear cows in Spiti dry up the dung and fill it in sacks. During winter, these sacks are laid out in the sheds where the cows live, which are called *khud*s. During snowfall, these sacks give protection to the cows from the cold. After winters, this cow dung is used as manure in the fields. As the cost of cultivation is low and the yield in the fields is high, it became an inspiration to all of India for natural farming. The PM described how this symbiosis was innate to the local culture of Spiti through a traditional folk song, 'Chhapra Majhi Chhapra', which means mutual cooperation.

Mutual cooperation to ensure food security and sustainable living is not relevant only to a single local community or a region but now spans across borders and continents. The United Nations (UN) resolution to mark 2023 as the International Year of Millets, which has resulted in more than 70 countries joining India to popularize millets, is a sign of how global cooperation on agriculture is imperative for sustainable farming. This has given culinary diplomacy a whole new dimension.

Revealing in *Mann Ki Baat* how visiting heads of states and heads of governments are being treated to a millets menu during official banquets, luncheons and dinners, PM Modi highlighted the growing popularity of India's coarse grains.

> Millets, coarse grains, have been a part of our agriculture, culture and civilization since ancient times. Millets are mentioned in our Vedas, and similarly, they are also mentioned in Purananuru and Tolkāppiyam. If you go to any part of the country, you will definitely find different types of millets in the food of the people there. In millets too, just like our culture, a lot of diversity is found. Jowar, Bajra, Ragi, Sawan, Kangni, Cheena, Kodo, Kutki, Kuttu, all these are just millets.[1]

---

[1] "PM's Address in the 92nd Episode of "Mann Ki Baat"", *PMIndia*, 28 August 2022, https://tinyurl.com/5dmjsv2w. Accessed on 3 April 2023.

INNOVATION: FROM LAB TO LAND

India is the world's largest producer of millets, *Mann Ki Baat* has been at the forefront of creating awareness and championing innovations to make millet consumption into a mass movement for sustainable food security. Drawing the attention of listeners to the trendy innovations with millets being attempted by the food-processing sector, PM Modi spoke at length in August 2022 on millets as a superfood that can help reduce the risks of obesity, diabetes, hypertension and heart- and liver-related ailments. With food start-ups attempting innovative products based on millets, like millet cookies, pancakes, dosa and even energy bars, a breakfast revolution of sorts seems imminent. The championing of millets within the food chain in India and across the world is bound to make an impact on the environment, by bringing down the pressure on water tables with increased millets farming.

Mann Ki Baat has seen several other agri-innovations receive national spotlight. The development of new breeds of wheat and rice that specially contain Vitamin D by Hyderabad's Chintala Venkat Reddy has not only received a patent from the World Intellectual Property Organization, Geneva, but has emerged as a godsend for those with a deficiency of Vitamin D. Urugen Futsog from Ladakh, who is growing about 20 crops organically in a cyclic way (by utilizing the waste of one crop as manure for the next crop), has become a role model for farmers across India. Kamraj Bhai Choudhary from Patan district in Gujarat has developed high-yield variety of drumstick seeds, also known as Sargava or Moringa, and is selling his produce across India. In response to the growing popularity of import of chia seeds, Harishchandra of Barabanki in Uttar Pradesh has begun cultivating chia seeds to help reduce their imports, while contributing to the self-reliant India campaign. Creating wealth from agricultural waste, Murugesan from Madurai has made a machine to make ropes from banana waste, thus, solving issues of waste disposal.

Food innovation is rapidly becoming a driving force that not only acknowledges India's rich biodiversity but also plays a crucial role in its conservation. The Himalayan fig or bedu, found in Uttarakhand, is drawing national attention for its nutritional and medicinal value. Several commercial products like jams, chutneys and pickles, including a dry fruits version of the fig, have emerged. *Mann Ki Baat*'s focus on the fig went beyond its nutritional aspects to how it has become a part of the digital economy with the launch of an online e-marketplace called 'Pahari Fig', opening up a new source of income for farmers.

Documenting the rich biodiversity of India and promoting natural wellness products based on herbs has emerged as a citizen-led initiative, with *Mann Ki Baat* bringing to light individual efforts across India. Patayat Sahu, who lives in Nandol, Kalahandi, Odisha, has grown medicinal plants on 1.5 acres of his land and documenting them. Deori village near Ranchi has over 40 women cultivating aloe vera, and is, thus, known as the Aloe Vera Village. This village is not just making money from the sale of aloe vera to companies making sanitizers, but also history.

With start-ups in the field of medicinal plants, an incubator by the name of Medi-Hub TBI is operational in Anand, Gujarat. In a very short time, this incubator has supported the business ideas of 15 entrepreneurs. These include women entrepreneurs such as Sudha Chebrolu, who is developing innovative herbal formulations, and Subhashree, who is working on home and car fresheners using a herbal terrace garden to grow more than 400 medicinal herbs. Additionally, a comic book character called

Professor Ayushman is also being used to promote the usefulness of healthy medicinal plants like aloe vera, tulsi, amla, giloy, neem, ashwagandha and brahmi. Overall, the immense potential of the Indian biodiversity is being leveraged to diversify farm incomes.

This shift beyond traditional farming with novel initiatives in agriculture is continuously creating new avenues for self-employment. The story of the two brothers, Bilal Ahmed Sheikh and Munir Ahmed Sheikh, is an example worthy of emulation. Having set up a vermicomposting unit at their home, they use the bio-fertilizer produced to boost agriculture and generate employment opportunities. About 3,000 quintals of vermicompost is produced from their units that employ around 15 workers. The Sheikh brothers have emerged as job creators, as envisioned by PM Modi on *Mann Ki Baat*.

Adversity brings out the best in human beings. The once-in-a-century pandemic was no exception, with citizens going out of their way to help fellow citizens through out-of-the-box thinking and commonplace innovations. Zaitoona Begum, a Kashmiri woman sarpanch of Chauntliwaar in Ganderbal, decided that her panchayat would fight the battle against Covid-19 and, along with that, create income opportunities. She distributed free masks and free ration in the vicinity. At the same time, she also distributed crop seeds and apple saplings so that people were not subjected to inconvenience in farming and horticulture.

Prime Minister Modi recalled more such instances:

In Bishunpur, Jharkhand, more than thirty groups are collectively cultivating lemongrass. It takes four months for lemongrass to mature and its oil fetches a decent price in the market. These days, this product is much in demand. I also wish to refer to two regions of the country—both are hundreds of kilometers apart; yet are contributing in making India self-reliant in their own unique, novel ways. One is Ladakh; the other is Kutch. The mere mention of Leh-Ladakh creates images of picturesque valleys, mountain heights and whiffs of fresh air. On the other hand, reference to Kutch draws images of an unending desert with no vegetation in sight. In Ladakh, a distinct fruit called chooli or apricot also known as Khubani is grown. This produce has the capacity to transform the economy of the area. But unfortunately, vagaries of supply chains and weather are some of the formidable challenges it keeps facing. To reduce spoilage to the minimum, a new innovation has been adopted for use. This is a dual system, called solar apricot dryer and space heater. This desiccates apricots, other fruits and vegetables as per requirement; that too in a hygienic manner. Earlier, when apricots used to be dried in the vicinity of farms, there would be spoilage, besides loss of quality of fruit on account of dust and rainwater. On the other side, these days, farmers of Kutch are making commendable efforts in the cultivation of dragon fruit. Many people are perplexed when they hear Kutch and dragon fruit together. But, today, many farmers there have taken to this activity. Many innovations are taking place for enhancing fruit quality, productivity and yield. I have been told that the popularity of dragon fruit is constantly increasing, especially usage in breakfast has increased considerably. The farmers of Kutch have resolved that the country should not import dragon fruit and this is what self-reliance is all about.[2]

---

[2] PM's Address in the 14th Episode of "Mann Ki Baat 2.0'", *PMIndia* 26 July 2020, https://tinyurl.com/mruv4x56. Accessed on 3 April 2023.

However, one of the most innovative initiatives to figure prominently on *Mann Ki Baat*—that triangulates sustainable farming, food security and natural conservation—is bee farming. Farmers across India have taken to it, and it is fast emerging as the foundation of a Honey Revolution (also known as the Sweet Revolution), in the country. People in Gurdum, Darjeeling, with its steep mountains and treacherous terrain, have found a new source of income through honeybee farming. The organic honey of the Sundarbans in West Bengal is in great demand within India and overseas, while Banaskantha in Gujarat has become a major centre for honey production with lakhs of rupees in annual income. In Yamunanagar, Haryana, farmers are producing several hundred tons of honey annually to boost the national production to 1.25 lakh tons, contributing to the growing export of food products.

Elaborating on how this agri-innovation has byproducts beyond honey, Modi spoke on self-reliance and the need to cut imports.

Friends, honey bee farming does not lead to income solely from honey, but bee wax is also a very big source of income. There is demand for bee wax in everything—pharmaceutical, food, textile and cosmetic industries. Our country currently imports bee wax, but our farmers are now rapidly transforming this situation…that is, in a way contributing in the 'Atmanirbhar Bharat' campaign. Today, the whole world is looking at Ayurveda and natural health products. In such a situation, the demand for honey is increasing even more rapidly. I wish more and more farmers of our country to join bee farming along with their farming. This will lead to an increase in the income of the farmers too and will also sweeten their lives![3]

---

[3]"PM's address in the 75th Episode of "Mann Ki Baat"', *PMIndia,* 28 March

Mann Ki Baat's championing of food innovation and production extends well beyond farms, forests and mountains and dives deep into the new opportunities being created by the Blue Revolution. One such example is that of the youth from Bihar who has started cultivating pearls. This has not only resulted in enhanced income from the activity but has spurred migrant labourers returning from other states to receive training in Muzaffarpur, Begusarai and Patna, thus creating avenues for self-reliance. Remunerative alternatives have emerged with newer innovations and techniques. Bijay Shanti of Manipur, who launched a start-up to develop thread from the lotus stem, has initiated new opportunities in the fields of lotus farming and textile, and has become a talking point on *Mann Ki Baat*. Yet another Bijay, this time from Odisha, enthralled listeners with his initiative in Kendrapara to raise a 25-acre mangrove forest on the outskirts of his village to protect against nature's fury and to preserve the biodiversity along the coastline.

A NEW WAVE OF ECONOMIC INDEPENDENCE

Amplifying best practices in agriculture and new means to boost farm income, *Mann Ki Baat* has, over the years, educated its listeners on a vast range of subjects, from drip irrigation to food processing. Sharing the success of Kanwar Chauhan, a farmer from Sonepat in Haryana, in creating a farmers' produce organization that facilitated sale of produce directly to end customers by eliminating middlemen, *Mann Ki Baat* brought to fore concrete examples to boost farm income.

2021, https://tinyurl.com/79ac55ky. Accessed on 3 April 2023.

Today, the farmers of the village are earning rupees two and a half to three lakhs per acre annually by cultivating sweet corn and baby corn. Not only this, more than 60 farmers of this village, through construction of net house and poly house are producing various varieties of tomato, cucumber and capsicum and earning from 10 to 12 lakh rupees per acre every year.[4]

Dwelling on the freedom enjoyed by the farmers of Sonepat to sell directly, bypassing oppressive monopolies of middlemen, *Mann Ki Baat* brought a rare economic focus to its listeners to emphasize how the right to make economically prudent choices was the foundation of progress. By highlighting the efforts of Shree Swami Samarth Farmer Producer Company Ltd—a farmer producer's organization that helps about 4,500 farmers from nearly 70 villages in Pune and Mumbai—the programme explained how the freedom to sell and the right to choose had extended well beyond marketing of only fruits and vegetables to that of all produce, ranging from paddy and wheat to mustard and sugarcane. These farmers sell directly at the weekly markets established by the organization. Similarly, a farmers' collective in Tamil Nadu purchased hundreds of metric tons of vegetables and fruits from nearby villages during the lockdown, and supplied a vegetable combo kit to the city of Chennai.

Abdul Majid Wani, a resident of Shar area of Tral in Pulwama, is selling his geographical indication (GI)-tagged saffron through e-trading with the help of the National Saffron Mission at the trading centre in Pampore. Many people like him are involved

---

[4]"PM's Address in the 16th Episode of "Mann Ki Baat 2.0"", *PMIndia*, 27 September 2020, https://tinyurl.com/ytjkz367. Accessed on 3 April 2023.

in this activity in Kashmir. Dwelling on history, culture and technology has highlighted how economic freedom to farmers can become an instrument of soft power, taking Indian brands far and wide.

> Saffron has been associated with Kashmir for centuries. Kashmiri saffron is mainly grown in places like Pulwama, Budgam and Kishtwar. In May this year, the Kashmiri saffron was given the Geographical Indication Tag or GI tag. Through this, we want to make Kashmiri saffron a globally popular brand. [...] You will be delighted to know that after obtaining the GI Tag certificate, Kashmiri saffron was launched in a supermarket in Dubai. Now its exports will get a boost. This will further strengthen our efforts to build an Atmanirbhar Bharat. Farmers growing saffron will be especially benefited by this. Next time you decide to buy saffron, think of buying saffron of Kashmir! [5]

Another instance of this wave of economic independence sweeping the country comes from Rampura village of Banaskantha in Gujarat.

> Ismail Bhai wanted to do farming, but, now, as is the general attitude towards farming, his family raised eyebrows on the thoughts of Ismail Bhai! Ismail Bhai's father was into farming, but in that, he often incurred losses. Hence the father dissuaded; yet despite family members discouraging, Ismail Bhai decided that he would certainly take up farming. Ismail Bhai had resolved that he would dispel the notion

---

[5] PM's Address in the 19th Episode of "Mann Ki Baat 2.0", *PMIndia*, 27 December 2020, https://tinyurl.com/2rru3d4k. Accessed on 3 April 2023.

of farming being a loss-making activity and change the situation as well. He started farming, albeit using new methods and innovative techniques. Using drip irrigation, he cultivated potatoes, and today his potatoes are his hallmark. He is growing potatoes that are of very high quality. Ismail Bhai directly sells these potatoes to large companies; the middle men are just out of the question. And the result, he is earning handsome profits. He now has repaid all the debts of his father. And do you know the most significant fact? Today, Ismail Bhai is helping hundreds of farmers in his region. He is changing their lives too.[6]

Mann Ki Baat's steady focus on farmers' methods from drip irrigation to soil health, has had an impact on productivity over nine years, with several milestones marked along the way. In February 2017, complimenting the hard work of the farmers that had resulted in a record production of food grains, PM Modi informed his listeners about the 2,700 lakh tonnes of food grains produced across India. This was 8 per cent more than the last record set by our farmers. The cultivation of various pulse crops also found particular mention. Noting the vast spread of pulse crop cultivation across 290 lakh hectares of land, PM Modi reminded his listeners how farming in India was, primarily, a social cause and, secondarily, a commercial venture, with the poorest of the poor being the beneficiaries of protein nutrition from pulses.

This record output meant that in 2021, 80 crore underprivileged citizens were provided free ration during the Covid-19 pandemic.

---

[6]"PM's Address in the 16th Episode of "Mann Ki Baat 2.0"", *PMIndia*, 27 September 2020, https://tinyurl.com/ytjkz367. Accessed on 3 April 2023.

The Indian Railways emerged as a key enabler of the food supply chain, establishing linkages between farmers and markets. Jackfruits from Agartala were brought to Guwahati by rail before being flown to London along with the Shahi Litchi of Bihar. Similarly, mangoes from Vizianagaram found their way to the markets in Delhi. From east to west and from north to south, Kisan Rail transported nearly 2 lakh tonnes of produce, including fruits, vegetables and grains, at a very low cost.

Going beyond agriculture, PM Modi also highlighted a traditional element of rural life that has played a supportive role in farming—animal husbandry. Expressing concern on the low number of animals and amount of milk production in India, when compared to many other countries, he raised the issue of increasing milk productivity (on a per animal basis) by adapting traditional practices to new scientific methods and technologies. The occasion for this conversation was the launch of a TV channel, DD Kisan, dedicated to agriculture and related areas, perhaps one of its kind in the world.

UNDERSTANDING SYMBIOTIC CONNECTIONS

Making the innate symbiotic connection between nutrition and the Earth, *Mann Ki Baat* marked World Soil Day in 2017 to bring into focus the connection of the food chain in the subterranean ecosystem.

> This concern was touched upon a long time ago in our culture and that is why we are aware of the significance of soil since ancient times. In our culture, there have been efforts to foster a feeling of devotion and gratitude towards our farms, our soil among the people and at the same time scientific

farming methods and techniques have been adopted which provide nutrients to the soil. In the life of the farmer of this country both aspects have been important—reverence to his soil and preserving and nurturing it scientifically.[7]

Soil health best practices rooted in traditions, along with farmers of Tooh village (in Bhoranj block of Hamirpur district in Himachal Pradesh) adopting modern ways, was the subject of *Mann Ki Baat* in November 2017. Recalling how these farmers were earlier using chemical fertilizers indiscriminately, which deteriorated the soil health and resulted in reduced produce and lower income, PM Modi raised awareness on the importance of soil testing. These farmers took expert advice on the quantity of fertilizers, micro-nutrients and organic fertilizers to be used in the Rabi season of 2016–17 and increased their wheat production per acre by three to four times and their income by ₹4,000–6,000 per acre.

Soil health cards have since become an essential aid to farmers across India for sustainable agriculture that nurtures the Earth, rather than destroy it. Noting that more than 10 crore soil health cards had been issued, PM Modi invoked the innately Indian ethic of worshipping the Earth as the mother, to caution against the use of chemical fertilizers indiscriminately.

From celebrating sparrows to the return of cheetahs, *Mann Ki Baat* has been a constant reminder of the symbiotic connection between food, farms, nature and biodiversity. From the Asiatic lions of Gir to the Mudhol Hounds, both native and migratory species have received their due on the programme. The coexistence with animals, birds and nature has been a consistent

---

[7]'English Rendering of PM's Mann Ki Baat Programme on All India Radio', *PMIndia,* 26 November 2017, https://tinyurl.com/skftx33e. Accessed on 3 April 2023.

theme on *Mann Ki Baat*, which is illustrated by the example of Jagat Bhai from Gujarat, who had written a book titled, *Save the Sparrows*.

Marking noted Indian ornithologist Salim Ali's 125th birth anniversary, PM Modi, in his characteristic style, evoked two instances to make the case for preserving biodiversity and taking care of wildlife. First was a huge campaign launched under the aegis of Burhani Foundation, with 52,000 bird feeders to save the sparrows during the centenary year of Syedna Saheb, (the religious leader of Dawoodi Bohra Community. The second instance was of a riveting song by Bharat Ratna Bhupen Hazarika celebrating the one-horned rhinoceri as an integral part of Assamese culture. The song, while describing the lush green surroundings of Kaziranga, the abode of elephants and tigers, muses how the Earth watches the one-horned rhinoceri and listens to the melodious chirping of birds. By highlighting how the rhinoceri are also seen in the Moonga and Eri dresses woven on Assam's world-famous handlooms, PM Modi noted the steady decrease in the hunting of rhinoceri in Assam through emphasis on the campaign against the poaching of rhinoceri.

He reiterated the manner in which India's biodiversity inspires, captivates and motivates:

> We are surrounded by many such mysteries, which are still undiscovered. To discover such a phenomenal enigma calls for fierce detective passion.
>
> The great Tamil poetess Avvaiyar writes: Kattat Kemaavoon Kalladaru Udgadvu, Kaddat Kamiyan Adva Kalladar Olaaadu.
>
> This means, what we know is but just a handful of sand; what we do not know is like a universe in itself. Similar is

the case with the biodiversity of this country. The more you know, the more you realize the magnitude of what you do not know. Our biodiversity too is a unique treasure for the entire human kind. We have to preserve it, conserve it and explore further.[8]

Mann Ki Baat symbolizes India's vast geographical diversity, encompassing the various challenges and opportunities that arise from it. From highlighting mountain flora to diving deep into India's marine life, PM Modi's dialogue with India has straddled valleys, crossed deserts and spanned plateaus. His conversation with the nation, on a creed of ecological consciousness rooted in Indian cultural values, has inspired change on a national scale in the face of rapid development. Consistently threading the needle of the conversation through innately local values of natural preservation and conservation, *Mann Ki Baat* has given a new hope to a whole generation of farmers and agri-entrepreneurs to think big and secure India's farm and forest future.

---

[8]"PM's Address in the 9th Episode of "Mann Ki Baat 2.0"", *PMIndia*, 23 February 2020, https://tinyurl.com/4eb2juum. Accessed on 3 April 2020.

CHAPTER 8

RENEWED COMMITMENT TO CLEANLINESS AND CONSERVATION

Several decades from now, when the history of *Mann Ki Baat* is written, two initiatives aspiring to bring about mass behavioural change in Indian society will stand out for the scale of their imagination, breadth of aspiration and depth of impact. It is no accident that both these flagship initiatives draw inspiration from two iconic personalities of modern India—Mahatma Gandhi and Dr B.R. Ambedkar. While Gandhi as the inspiration for Swachh Bharat Abhiyan is well understood, Ambedkar as the inspiration for Jal Shakti Abhiyan is little known. In the 1930s and 1940s, when only roads and railways were being talked about in India, Ambedkar envisioned a network of ports and waterways to advance the idea of water power as 'nation power'. His emphasis on utilization of water for the development of the nation was the genesis of different river valley authorities and various water-related commissions over the decades.

Realizing Ambedkar's vision to harness the potential of water through ports and waterways has become a mass movement over the past nine years, with conservation and development marching hand in hand. In 2023, with the launch of the world's longest river cruise, a discussion of the intrinsic connection among water conservation, riverways development and environmental cleanliness on *Mann Ki Baat* has caught the attention of the nation.

Underpinning this mammoth task to conserve water and develop water bodies required a creative melding of Ambedkar's vision of a modern India with the ancient ethos of revering water, which draws inspiration from the Rig Veda's 'Apah Suktam':

आपो हिष्ठा मयो भुवः, स्था न ऊर्जे दधातन, महे रणाय चक्षसे, यो वः शिवतमो रसः, तस्य भाजयतेह नः, उषतीरिव मातरः ।

Meaning that it is water which is the life force and also, the source of energy. Please bless us like a mother and may your blessings continue on to be showered upon us.[1]

It is this ancient practice of worshipping water that has evolved into cultures around the great rivers of India.

Pibanti Naddhah, Swayameva Naambha...meaning that rivers do not drink their own water...they give it away altruistically. For us, rivers are not mere physical entities; for us a river is a living unit...and that is exactly why we refer to rivers as Mother! Numerous festivals, festive occasions, functions of ours, occasions to rejoice take place in the very laps of these mothers.[2]

---

[1] 'PM's Address in "Mann Ki Baat 2.0" Programme on All India Radio', *PMIndia*, 30 June 2019, https://tinyurl.com/3hhx3ecs. Accessed on 3 April 2023.
[2] 'PM's Address in the 81st Episode of "Mann Ki Baat"', *PMIndia*, 26 September 2021, https://tinyurl.com/rxfxjpd9. Accessed on 3 April 2023.

With only 8 per cent of the water received from rains being harvested in the entire year, one of the first challenges undertaken by PM Modi's government was to ensure *janbhagidari* (participation of the people) and *janshakti* (people's power) to make rainwater harvesting a mass movement. While the new Ministry of Jal Shakti enabled faster decision-making on all subjects related to water, PM Modi, through *Mann Ki Baat*, spoke about the need to make local governments stakeholders in this mission. He reached out to sarpanchs and gram pradhans across the country to convene a meeting of gram sabhas, focussed on the agenda of saving water and harvesting rains, and a mass movement started to take shape.

With crores of people making *shramdaan* (voluntary contributions of labour) across thousands of panchayats, water conservation efforts got a nationwide boost. This gave much-needed visibility to the efforts of government and social service organizations in rejuvenating rivers throughout the country. Giving examples of Vellore and Tiruvannamalai of Tamil Nadu, PM Modi highlighted how public participation in the form of digging canals, constructing check dams and recharge wells had resulted in the revival of the river Naganadhi.

The PM also recalled how various Indian scriptures distinctly disapproved of polluting rivers. He emphasized the cultural significance of cleaning and repairing riverbanks and ghats by giving the example of Chhath (observed in Bihar and eastern Uttar Pradesh). Listeners were also made aware of the tradition of Jal Jhilani Ekadashi, which is synonymous with modern day rainwater harvesting.

Foremost among these efforts to rejuvenate rivers by invoking culture and traditions was the Namami Gange Mission, which became a mass movement to save the river Ganga.

When Namami Gange is being referred to, one thing is certain to draw your attention…especially that of the youth. These days, a special e-auction is being held. This electronic auction pertains to gifts presented to me by people from time to time. The money that accrues through this e-auction is dedicated solely to the Namami Gange campaign.[3]

Prime Minister Modi also informed listeners of the recent revival of the Sabarmati River after it had dried up over decades. With the linkages from Narmada to Sabarmati and the development of its riverfront as one of the undertakings, the mission to rejuvenate India's rivers extended from the northern plains to the Tamil Nadu coast. Spiritual gurus associated with various religious traditions also conducted campaigns to plant trees along the riverbanks, prevent dirty water from flowing into rivers and renovate ghats.

INVOKING HISTORY ALONGSIDE MODERNITY

Mann Ki Baat has invoked history alongside modernity to make water conservation and rejuvenation a mass movement, which is demonstrated by the construction of the stepwells in Gujarat and Rajasthan as well as by the modern-day dams conceived by Sir M. Visvesvaraya. Porbandar, the birth place of Mahatma Gandhi, was a role model with its 200-year-old underground water tank that was directly recharged with rainwater. Celebrated poetess Mahadevi Varma, who wrote about storing water in earthen bowls for birds in the summer, was also an inspiration. The temple carvings of Tamil Nadu merit special mention for depicting irrigation system, water conservation methods and drought management. Stone carvings

---

[3]Ibid.

in Tamil Nadu at Mannarkovil, Cheranmahadevi, Kovilpatti and Pudukkottai, with their educational messages on water conservation, remind us of a tradition that goes back centuries.

Consequently, the mission to conserve water gained momentum through *Mann Ki Baat* with different state governments, from Telangana to Chhattisgarh, pitching in with their own initiatives. The farmers of Hiware Bazar Gram Panchayat in Ahmednagar district of Maharashtra walked the talk on water conservation by changing their farming pattern to less water-intensive crops, while those in Gorwa Gram Panchayat in Dewas district of Madhya Pradesh built more than 20 farm ponds to recharge the groundwater table. In Kerala, 7,000 workers worked hard for 70 days to revive the Kuttamperoor River. In Uttar Pradesh's Fatehpur district, twin rivers Sasuri–Khaderi, which had dried up, were revived with the participation of 40–45 villages. The sarpanch of Lupung Panchayat of Katkamsandi block in Hazaribagh district of Jharkhand shared an innovative competition for 'raising a water temple' in every village to motivate water conservation. In Vellore, Tamil Nadu, 20,000 women had taken it upon themselves to revive the river Nag.

In a feat reminiscent of Bhagiratha's endeavour from ancient Indian epics, the Aara-Keram village (under the Ormanjhi block near Ranchi in Jharkhand), with the industry of the villagers, was able to change the course of a mountain spring, stopping soil erosion and crop damage. In particular, Meghalaya was praised by PM Modi as the first Indian state to formulate a water policy. The mass movement that water conservation has become has led to a steady rush of efforts from the revival of the Kalyani river in Uttar Pradesh's Barabanki to tree plantation efforts in Uttarakhand's Bageshwar.

Prime Minister Modi hailed this citizen-led innovation, where traditional methods met modern engineering, to take advantage of the community's industry:

I consider water conservation as a form of service to the country. You too must have seen, many of us are taking this pious work as their responsibility [sic]. One such person is Satchidanand Bharti ji of Pauri Garhwal, Uttarakhand. Bharti ji is a teacher and he has imparted very good education to the people through his deeds. Today, due to his hard work, the huge water crisis in the Ufrainkhal area of Pauri Garhwal has come to an end. Where people used to pine for water, today there is continuous supply of water throughout the year.

Friends, in the hills there exists a traditional method of water conservation, which is called Chalkhal. That is, it involves digging a big pit to collect water. Bharti ji also added some new methods to this tradition. He regularly got small and big ponds dug. Due to this, not only the hills of Ufrainkhal turned green, but the problem of drinking water of the people was also solved. You will be surprised to know that Bharti ji has got more than 30 thousand such water tanks constructed. 30 thousand! This monumental work of his continues even today and is inspiring many people.

Friends, similarly the people of Andhav village in Banda district of UP [Uttar Pradesh] have also made an innovative effort and have given a very interesting name to their campaign—'Khet ka pani khet mein, gaon ka pani gaon mein'. Under this campaign, high bunds have been raised in several hundred bighas of fields of the village.

As a result, rain water started collecting in the field, and started percolating into the ground. Now, these people are also planning to plant trees on the bunds of the fields. That is, now farmers will get all three—water, trees and money![4]

Friends, the people of Ghaziabad in UP know Ramveer Tanwar as the 'Pond Man'. Ramveer ji was doing a job after completing his mechanical engineering. However, such a sense of devotion for cleanliness ignited in his mind that he left his job and started cleaning ponds. So far, Ramveer ji has revived many ponds by cleaning them.[5]

DECODING INDIA'S BIGGEST BEHAVIOURAL CHANGE

Mann Ki Baat also became a mass outreach platform to make the connection between water conservation and cleanliness early on, thus heralding the biggest behavioural change in the history of modern India—Swachh Bharat Abhiyan. The mass movement towards cleanliness was as much about conservation as it was about eliminating open defecation. *Mann Ki Baat*, from its very first episode, was dedicated to the cause of cleanliness and pursued it with a relentlessness unseen and unheard of since India became independent.

To PM Modi, cleanliness is a deeply personal cause and it is to the credit of his creative genius that it has the same importance for lakhs of Indians, including children. Indeed, the pursuit of

---

[4]"PM's address in the 78th Episode of "Mann Ki Baat"", *PMIndia*, 27 June 2021, https://tinyurl.com/2s35k5y7. Accessed on 7 April 2023.
[5]"PM's Address in the 82nd Episode of "Mann Ki Baat"", *PMIndia*, 24 October 2021, https://tinyurl.com/ycywz3wx. Accessed on 3 April 2023.

cleanliness encompasses numerous social prejudices, historical discrimination, gender vulnerabilities, public health concerns and the significant developmental divide that must be overcome in order to forge New India, unified in its commitment to hygiene, equity and progress.

Leading by example, he has sought to make cleanliness a way of life beyond the four walls of home, which has resulted in citizen-led efforts towards cleanliness. The mission to build toilets and eliminate open defecation drew strength from Indian culture and traditions to spur communities to develop sanitation infrastructure. By 2019, when *Mann Ki Baat* marked its fifth anniversary, the mission had accomplished a target of 5.5 lakh villages across 600 districts of India, bringing 9 crore households access to toilets. Such was the enthusiasm that in December 2018 alone, 50 lakh toilets were built under the Clean Beautiful Toilet and Shining Toilet contests.[6]

Many unsung heroes of Swachh Bharat Abhiyan have been the mainstay of *Mann Ki Baat* since its very inception. Dileep Singh Malviya of Bhojpura village from Sehore district in Madhya Pradesh donated his masonry labour, free of cost, to construct toilets, while Chandrakant Kulkarni, a pensioner from Pune, donated almost a third of his pension worth ₹2.6 lakh from June 2015 to September 2019 to the Swachh Bharat Kosh through 52 post-dated cheques. Sixteen-year-old Mallamma from Koppal in Karnataka, who adopted the Gandhian protest of Satyagraha, emerged as a role model for the mission. Mallamma elaborated on her unique Satyagraha in July 2016:

---

[6]'Over 5 Lakh Villages Declared ODF: Modi', *Business Standard*, 27 January 2019, https://tinyurl.com/2p99vcyy. Accessed on 19 April 2023.

The slogans—Toilet Our Right and Toilet a Symbol of Self-Esteem—motivated me to make a demand. Since ours is a joint family, my mother's budget was limited. When I told her about the government's subsidy of ₹15,000 for dalit families, she would say, toilet is for the rich. That's when I decided to shun food till my family came around.[7]

These people provided inspiration to the mission to clean India even across the most difficult of terrains. Brave soldiers embarked on the Swachh Siachen initiative to clean up the glacier. With the segregation and management of garbage, more than 130 tons of waste was removed from the glacier and its surrounding area's fragile ecosystem that is home to rare species like the snow leopard, ibex and brown bear. The cleanliness campaign also ensured clean water for those who live in low-lying areas and use the water of rivers like Nubra and Shyok.

Pradeep Sangwan's Healing Himalayas initiative has resulted in tons of plastic being cleared from prominent treks, spiritual sites and temple premises in the mountains, as well as raised awareness about the health of the environment. Explaining how *Mann Ki Baat* helped him sustain his campaign, he says, 'The programme has helped this initiative reach more people and helped us engage with them with seriousness. I look forward to engaging and collaborating with many others who are working at the grassroots in India through *Mann Ki Baat* so we can join forces to make a difference to the country.'[8]

There are many others who are making a difference like

---

[7]Menasinakai, Sangamesh, 'Koppal Girl Fasts for 3 Days for a Toilet in Village Home', *The Times of India*, 16 July 2016, https://tinyurl.com/yc66pdaa. Accessed on 19 April 2023.
[8]As told to Doordarshan in March 2023.

Pradeep. Newly-weds Anudeep and Minusha cleared 800 kg of waste from Someshwara beach in Karnataka. Rahul Maharana's efforts to clear plastics from pilgrim sites in Puri, Odisha, brought a message of cleanliness to holy sites, while Chandrakishore Patil's constant endeavour to prevent garbage and plastics from accumulating on the bank of the Godavari in Nashik, Maharashtra, underscored how the water mission and the cleanliness mission were deeply interlinked.

Coastal cleanliness on the Bay of Bengal coast assumed tremendous significance with tourist destinations taking the lead. Scuba divers, who impart training in Visakhapatnam, were getting obstructed by plastic bottles and pouches on their way back from sea on Mangamaripeta beach. They took it upon themselves to deep dive and clear the garbage. Over a two-week period, more than 4,000 kg of plastic waste from the sea was removed by the divers, with the local fishermen lending a helping hand. This gave a tremendous boost to the goal of plastic-free India publicized through *Mann Ki Baat*. Visakhapatnam also saw an initiative to promote cloth bags instead of polythene with a campaign against single-use plastic products. Youth in Rajasthan started a campaign called Mission Beat Plastic, in which plastic and polythene have been removed from the forests of Ranthambore.

Saluting the efforts of these unsung heroes and urging citizens to make their contributions to cleanliness, PM Modi said:

In Kottayam of Kerala there is an elderly divyang, N.S. Rajappan Sahab. Due to paralysis, Rajappan is incapable of walking, but this has not affected his commitment to cleanliness. For the past several years he has been going by boat in Vembanad lake and taking out the plastic bottles thrown into the lake. Think, how great Rajappan ji's thought is! Taking inspiration from Rajappan ji, we too should, wherever possible, make our contribution to cleanliness.[9]

VALUE FROM WASTE

The waste-to-wealth mantra that emerged from the cleanliness mission has inspired several instances of innovation and grassroots action. With cities vying to compete with each other in the annual cleanliness survey, it has also spurred urban rejuvenation. For instance, Indore has transformed itself by not just emerging as the cleanest city but by going one step ahead as a 'Water Plus City' to ensure no untreated waste water is dumped into the city's water bodies. Dr Rajendra Prasad Central Agricultural University, Bihar, along with the local Krishi Vigyan Kendra, evolved the Sukhet Model to reduce pollution in the villages. Under this model, dung and other household waste collected from farmers provides monetary incentives for cooking-gas cylinders, apart from generating vermicompost bio-fertilizer from the disposed garbage. Kanjirangal panchayat of Sivaganga district in Tamil Nadu is generating electricity from waste in their village with a capacity of 2 tonnes of waste per day. The electricity generated from this power plant is utilized for streetlights and other needs of the village.

Value from waste has inspired more innovations across India. One such example is that of St Teresa's College in Kochi, Kerala. Students of this college are making reusable toys in a

[9]"PM's Address in the 20th Episode of "Mann Ki Baat 2.0"", *PMIndia*, 31 January 2021, https://tinyurl.com/5yd6vcby. Accessed on 3 April 2023.

very creative manner. These students are converting old clothes, discarded wooden pieces, bags and boxes into toys like puzzles, cars and trains. Professor Srinivas Padakandla from Vijayawada, Andhra Pradesh, has created sculptures from automobile metal scrap. These huge sculptures made by him have been installed in public parks in an innovative experiment combining electronic and automobile waste recycling with creativity.

The PM drew the attention of his countrymen to the successful efforts related to waste-to-wealth:

> One such example is that of Aizwal, the capital of Mizoram. There is a beautiful river Chite Lui in Aizwal, which due to neglect for years, had turned into a heap of dirt and garbage. Efforts have started in the last few years to save this river. For this, local agencies, voluntary organizations and local people, together, are also running the Save Chite Lui action plan. This campaign of cleaning the river has also made an opportunity for wealth creation from waste. Actually, this river and its banks were full of plastic and polythene waste. The organization working to save the river, decided to build a road using this polythene, that is, the waste that came out of the river. From that, in a village in Mizoram, the state's first plastic road was built...that is cleanliness and development as well.
>
> Friends, one such effort has also been undertaken by the youth of Puducherry through their voluntary organizations. Puducherry is situated along the sea coast. A large number of people come to see the beaches and marine beauty there. But the pollution caused by plastic was also increasing on the sea coast of Puducherry, therefore, to save its sea, beaches and ecology, people here have started the 'Recycling for

Life' campaign. Today, thousands of kilograms of garbage is collected and segregated every day in Karaikal, Puducherry. The organic waste from that is made into compost; the rest of the matter is separated and recycled. Such efforts are not only inspiring, but also lend momentum to India's campaign against single use plastic.[10]

A close observer of the pivotal role played by *Mann Ki Baat* in advancing the twin missions of cleanliness and water conservation is Parameswaran Iyer, who served as the secretary to the Government of India in the Ministry of Drinking Water and Sanitation between 2016 and 2020. Reflecting on the impact of the programme in making villages across India ODF, Iyer attributes the effectiveness of the mission to PM Narendra Modi playing the role of the nation's chief executive and communicator-in-chief through his monthly radio dialogue with the citizens of India.

Noting how almost every episode has focussed on these twin missions, Iyer draws a direct linkage of the programme to the mass behavioural change observed across villages. Iyer singles out two specific instances that, in his view, were the direct outcome of PM Modi's calls to action through *Mann Ki Baat*. First was the manner in which Tata Trusts supported young professionals becoming district-level champions for the Zila Swachh Bharat Prerak programme in response to PM Modi's call to the corporate sector. Iyer notes their impact on the ground, as eyes and ears to the district collectors, pursuing the mission of making India's villages ODF.[11]

---

[10]'PM's Address in the 90th Episode of "Mann Ki Baat"', 26 June 2022, https://tinyurl.com/3m2e62sy. Accessed on 3 April 2023.

[11]In conversation with the author in March 2023.

A second instance that stands out, according to Iyer, was the role of *Mann Ki Baat* in attacking the stigma attached with building toilets within homes in rural India. The two-pit toilet design championed by Iyer and his team found a rare mention on the programme in February 2017, with bureaucrats rolling up their sleeves and getting their hands dirty to demonstrate how community action can help achieve the goal of ODF villages. A UN Children's Fund (UNICEF) study on the economic impact of ODF rural life estimated that rural households could save up to more than ₹50,000 a year through better health and hygiene, while real estate value also appreciated in the countryside because of improved sanitation.[12]

Undoubtedly, the profound impact of *Mann Ki Baat* on both the Swachh Bharat Abhiyan and the Jal Jeevan Mission is largely due to PM Modi personally making the case for mass behavioural change across India, month after month, over the span of the last nine years.

---

[12]'Economic Survey Takes Note of Positive Health and Economic Impact in ODF Areas', *Press Information Bureau*, 29 January 2018, https://tinyurl.com/y5b4bx8m. Accessed on 30 March 2023.

CHAPTER 9

THE TRUE SPIRIT OF CELEBRATION

Right from its inception of in 2014, the confluence of festivals, culture and arts and crafts, which keeps the eternal economic cycle of growth and development sustainable, has been the mantra of *Mann Ki Baat.*

With the move towards renewable sources of energy, culture and festivals were a reminder to listeners on how sustainable living was integral to traditions within most communities in India. Chhath, which is celebrated a few weeks after Diwali in eastern parts of India, exemplifies these traditional ethics. The PM reiterated how the tradition of worshipping the Sun connects culture and faith to nature, and highlighted the importance of sunlight in daily life:

Solar energy is a subject today in which the whole world is looking at its future and for India, the Sun God has not only been worshiped for centuries, but has also been the focus of our way of life. Today, India is combining its traditional experiences with modern science, that is why, today, we have become one of the largest countries to generate electricity from solar energy. How solar energy is changing the lives of the poor and middle class of our country is also a subject of study.[1]

With a focus on cleanliness of rivers, ghats and various sources of water at the community level, celebrating Chhath is as much about worshipping nature as it is about conserving its gifts—the water bodies. From local fruits to *thekua* (revered sweet offering made during Chhath Puja), many of the items used for worship are sourced from within the local community such as the *supli* (basket) made of bamboo and the earthen lamps. The observance creates a source of income for both farmers who grow grams and small entrepreneurs making *batasha*s (sugar cake sweetmeat), thus creating a virtuous cycle of sustainable consumption within the local community.

PM MODI'S *KAUSHALANJALI*

Celebrating traditional craftmanship to rediscover the cultural roots of sustainability, in August 2021, *Mann Ki Baat* dwelt at length on Vishwakarma Jayanti, the birthday of Vishwakarma who, within the Hindu pantheon, is regarded the divine architect and craftsman.

Bhagwan Vishwakarma is considered as a symbol of the creative power behind the genesis of the world. Whoever through their skill, builds an object...innovates... whether

---

[1]"PM's Address in the 94th Episode of "Mann Ki Baat"", *PMIndia*, 30 October 2022, https://tinyurl.com/yckbv623. Accessed on 6 April 2023.

it is sewing-embroidery, software or satellite, all this is a manifestation of Bhagwan Vishwakarma. Even though skill is being recognized in a new way in the world today, our sages and seers have emphasized on skill and scale for thousands of years. They have interlinked skill, talent, ability with faith, thereby making it a part of the philosophy of our lives. Our Vedas have also dedicated many sukta to Bhagwan Vishwakarma. Whichever great creations are there, whatever new and big works have been done, our scriptures ascribe them to Bhagwan Vishwakarma. It is in a way a symbol of the thought that whatever development and innovation is happening in the world happens only through skills. This is the very sentiment behind the birth anniversary of Bhagwan Vishwakarma and his worship. And this has been quoted in our scriptures too:

विश्वम कृत्–सन्म कर्म व्यापारो यस्य स: विश्वकर्मा

Meaning, the one who takes all efforts in the process of creating and building is a Vishwakarma. In the view of our scriptures, all the skilled, talented people around us engaged in the process of creation and building are the legacy of Bhagwan Vishwakarma.[2]

The PM also drew attention to the dire situation of traditional skills fading out. Listeners were sensitized on the need to preserve these traditional skills or *kaushalya*, given their impact on family life, social life and the life of the nation.

One such inspirational role model to feature on *Mann Ki Baat* is Yeldhi Hariprasad, a traditional weaver from Rajanna

---

[2]"PM's Address in the 80th Episode of "Mann Ki Baat", *PMIndia*, 29 August 2021, https://tinyurl.com/pkkrrp6u. Accessed on 6 April 2023.

Sircilla in Telangana, who handwove the G20 logo to mark India's Presidency.[3] Thanking him for the handwoven gift, PM Modi made an important observation on how many of these traditional skills rooted in a sustainable lifestyle were hereditary and needed to be preserved.

By giving the example of an effort from Nagaland, the PM emphasized the importance of ensuring that traditional knowledge is passed on across generations. The listeners were introduced to 'Lidi-Cro-U' through his explanation of how the people of Nagaland valued their skills and culture for a sustainable lifestyle. Undertaking the work of reviving beautiful facets of Naga culture, which were on the verge of being lost, Lidi-Cro-U had started the work of launching Naga music albums alongside conducting workshops related to folk music and dance. Imparting training in the traditional Nagaland style of apparel making, tailoring and weaving, using naturally sourced bamboo in the Northeast, Lidi-Cro-U's efforts are connecting youth with their culture while generating new employment opportunities for them.[4]

At the intersection of local culture and sustainable livelihoods lie the creativity of local arts and crafts, and the enterprise of community efforts such as self-help groups (SHGs). The Tharagaigal Kaivinai Porutkal Virpanai Angadi from Thanjavur, Tamil Nadu, bringing together 22 SHGs, has not only seen the rising sales of handicraft products like the Thanjavur doll and bronze lamps, but has also imbibed modern technology such as the GI to script a

---

[3]Kumarnath, K.V., 'The Weaver Who Gifted PM a Handwoven G20 Logo', *The Hindu Businessline*, 28 November 2022, https://tinyurl.com/r6dr3n2t. Accessed on 13 April 2023.

[4]Kalita, Kangkan, 'PM Narendra Modi Pat for Naga Lifestyle, Culture', *The Times of India*, 28 November 2022, https://tinyurl.com/4ytymdxv. Accessed on 13 April 2023.

new saga of women empowerment. Through this campaign, not only have the artisans got a fillip, but the women are also getting empowered through rising incomes.[5]

The state of Tamil Nadu was in the news when a team of tribal women in Anaikatti, Coimbatore, crafted 10,000 eco-friendly terracotta tea cups for export. Highlighting how villages of Tripura have ascended to the level of Bio-Village 2 with the focus on solar energy, biogas, beekeeping and bio-fertilizers, PM Modi introduced listeners to the Mission LiFE portal. Dedicated to protect the environment, the principle behind this portal was to promote skills that do not harm the environment.[6]

By calling for action to perpetuate these skills for future generations through knowledge sharing and skill development, PM Modi made the connection between culture and sustainable livelihoods giving the modern social context for Vishwakarma Jayanti. He recalled a century-old initiative of Lokmanya Bal Gangadhar Tilak that led to a cultural renaissance of sorts, with the public observation of Ganesh Chaturthi to put the spotlight on eco-friendly festivals. Tilak initiated communities into the celebration of the festival marking the birth of Lord Ganesh in eco-friendly ways, from making Ganesh idols using clay to celebrating the occasion with assorted leaves, flowers and fruits. This tradition of community observance of the festival deepened the spirit of nationalism more than a century ago. Observing its 125th anniversary in 2017, PM Modi called for a resolve to use eco-friendly clay Ganesh idols and to protect the environment,

---

[5]"Self-Help Group from Thanjavur Sends Gift to PM, Earns Praise from Him", *The Print*, 30 May 2022, https://tinyurl.com/477yayd5. Accessed on 13 April 2023.
[6]"PM Modi Shares Story of Terracotta Tea Cups, Tripura's Bio Village in @ Mann Ki Baat", *ANI*, 30 October 2022, https://tinyurl.com/yhhzyksb. Accessed on 13 April 2023.

while creating livelihoods for local artisans and artists involved in idol making.

Even today, our culture continues to motivate and inspire sustainable living in many different ways. Giving the example of an innovative cultural experiment from Udaipur, Rajasthan, PM Modi brought to the attention of the listeners how culture and conservation came together to save a centuries old stepwell. Sultan ki Baori, which was built by Rao Sultan Singh, had suffered abject neglect over the years. Reduced to a pile of garbage, the historic site of water conservation had become dilapidated and abandoned.

Seeing this sorry state, an enterprising group of youth resolved to rejuvenate the stepwell. They resolved to change the picture and destiny of Sultan ki Baori gave birth to an innovative mission. Titled Sultan se Sur-Tan, the mission caught the attention of communities and citizens with its rhythmic name. The group's effort to rejuvenate the stepwell was now linked to musical notes and melody. After cleaning Sultan's stepwell and decorating it, the group has since regaled audiences with musical performances. Drawing international attention, the innovative effort at conservation and climate action drawing from culture has set the tone for sustainable living.

FROM 'I' TO 'WE'

Prime Minister Modi advanced the idea of one spirit, linking the individual self to the whole society in a collective existence by reflecting on the entire journey of Indian festivals over the centuries, their widespread effect, the depths to which they have influenced society and their intimate connect with each individual. Explaining how, through festivals, holistic development was ensured across all strata of society, he underscored the subtle message of food sustainability embedded within festival observances.

He highlighted the significance of food restrictions and culinary traditions associated with Indian festivals by making linkages to seasons, crops harvested by the farmers and sustainable food habits that have evolved over time:

> Festivals have evoked a sense of responsibility towards everything, be it trees, plants, rivers, animals, mountains, birds, etc. Nowadays we observe Sunday as a holiday but in our older generations, labourers, fishermen and others from such sections of society used to observe holidays on New Moon, that is Amavasya and Full Moon, that is Poornima. And science has proved that on these days changes take place impacting the sea-water; other factors affect nature and these also influence the human mind. Thus, we had developed the tradition to observe our holidays also intertwined with the phenomena of the Universe keeping the scientific aspects in focus.[7]

In Indian culture, the relationship between society and nature is so intimate that they become indistinguishable from each other. Manifestations of this interconnection between society and nature are the many traditional calendars of India, dotted with festivals. The year-round festival calendar of India, tracing the movements of the celestial bodies, depicts a centuries-old bonding with nature and astronomical events at its heart. The movement of the Earth

---

[7]'PM's "Mann Ki Baat" Programme on All India Radio on 30 October 2016', *PMIndia,* 30 October 2016, https://tinyurl.com/bde7s8u6. Accessed on 6 April 2023.

with respect to the Moon and Sun determines the dates of various festivals with rich cultural diversity across calendar traditions. In many regions, the position of the planetary constellations determines the occurrence and celebration of festivals.

While Gudi Padwa, Cheti Chand, Ugadi and others are determined based on the lunar calendar, Puthandu, Vishu, Baisakhi, Poila Baisakh and Bihu are determined by the solar calendar traditions. The solstice and relative motion of the Sun inspire the harvest festivals of Lohri, Pongal, Makar Sankranti, Uttarayan, Magh Bihu and Maghi (as they are known in different parts), thus making January a special month across India. From traditional dances to the embers of Lohri symbolizing the joy of a bountiful harvest, skies dotted with colourful flying kites, playing traditional games and sports, and making sweets with sesame and jaggery—while exchanging the greeting phrase '*Til gur ghya aani gorgor bola*' (Take the sesame and jaggery, and speak sweetly)—this period marks the eternal relationship shared by crops, farming, village life and food sustainability.

From conserving water to preserving water bodies, PM Modi has reinforced the message of social values inherent within festival observances. Given the grand scale of these observances attracting visitors from across the globe, festivals such as the Kumbh are no longer just about the tidal upsurge of faith and reverence, but also about rejuvenating rivers and demonstrating to the world innately Indian values within the modern context of sustainability.

A celebration of spirituality and philosophy, the Kumbh has emerged as the confluence of faith and nationalism. Drawing individuals across the globe, its aesthetics and creativity are an inter-generational message of oneness of culture, sustainable living and spiritual introspection. The tradition of Kumbh has bloomed and flourished, signifying cultural heritage. It is a measure of its global importance that the UNESCO has added the Kumbh Mela to the list of Intangible Cultural Heritage of Humanity.[8]

Drawing the attention of ambassadors of many countries and sporting their national flags, the modern-day observance of the ancient Indian festival of Kumbh recorded footfalls from more than 150 countries, with its divinity spreading the colours of India's splendour throughout the world.[9] Speaking on how the Kumbh is a journey of self-discovery, PM Modi addressed the unique spiritual experiences during this ancient Indian festival. Highlighting the importance of cleanliness during the Kumbh, he once again broke social taboos to press upon his listeners the need to ensure sanitation alongside reverence.

Prime Minister Modi also used this opportunity to reinforce the cultural mantra of cleanliness during festivals. Noting how festivals and cleanliness are linked together, with preparations for every festival always beginning with cleaning in individual households, he recognized the need to lend it a social character beyond the four walls of the house. Public cleanliness through a sense of community ownership inspired by festivals was key to take the cleanliness campaign beyond homes and across villages, towns, cities, states and the entire country:

> One thing that all of us know very well is that wherever in India we go, whether to the home of the richest of the rich or to the humble dwelling of the poorest of the poor, during

---

[8]"Kumbh Mela', *Intangible Cultural Heritage*, https://tinyurl.com/2b56xshc. Accessed on 13 April 2023.
[9]"Foreign Delegation of 150 Countries Reaches at Prayagraj, Take Holy Bath at Sangam', *ANI*, 23 February 2019, https://tinyurl.com/2p842dcr. Accessed on 13 April 2023.

the Diwali festival we can see a cleanliness campaign going on in every household. Every nook and corner of the house is cleaned. The less privileged also put in all their efforts to clean their modest earthen utensils because it is Diwali time. Thus, Diwali also encompasses a campaign of cleanliness. But the need of the hour is that not only individual houses but the entire premises, all the neighbourhood, the whole village be cleaned. We have to expand and spread this habit and tradition.[10]

From eco-friendly immersion of Ganesh idols in Andhra Pradesh to eco-friendly pilgrimages to the holy sites in the Himalayas, with the Char Dham Yatra becoming the focus, *Mann Ki Baat* has looked at festivals to sustain the momentum on the key change initiatives of PM Modi.

Friends, just as a pilgrimage is important here; equally important is 'Teertha Sewa' as has been mentioned and I would also say that without 'Teertha Sewa', a pilgrimage is also incomplete. There are many people in Devbhoomi Uttarakhand who are engaged in the 'sadhana' of cleanliness and service.[11]

Mann Ki Baat's call to action for sustainable pilgrimages, alongside devotion and spirituality, extended well beyond the Char Dham to include Amarnath Yatra, Pandharpur Yatra and Jagannath Yatra, apart from the multitudes of village fairs and local festivals across India.

---

[10]'PM's "Mann Ki Baat" Programme on All India Radio on 30 October 2016', *PMIndia*, 30 October 2016, https://tinyurl.com/bde7s8u6. Accessed on 6 April 2023.
[11]'PM's Address in the 89th Episode of "Mann Ki Baat', *PMIndia*, 29 May 2022, https://tinyurl.com/p2fuxceh. Accessed on 6 April 2023.

Prime Minister Modi also spoke of the courage to do away with outdated traditions and on the need to transform the manner of celebrating festivals according to changing times and social mores. A fine example of culture as an instrument of societal change is the Pandharpur Wari that underwent a grand transformation on Ashadhi Ekadashi. Pandharpur is a holy town in the Solapur district of Maharashtra. About 15–20 days before Ashadhi Ekadashi, *warkari* or pilgrims start the Pandharpur Yatra on foot. This yatra is known as *Wari* and lakhs of warkaris join this. *Paduka*s (wooden foot wear) of great saints like Saint Dnyaneshwar and Saint Tukaram are placed in a *palki* (palanquin) and pilgrims begin their pilgrimage chanting *Vitthal, Vitthal,* the name of the presiding diety of Pandharpur and an incarnation of Vishnu. Pilgrims go for *darshan* (worship) of Vitthal, who is also known as Vithoba or Pandurang.

Educating *Mann Ki Baat* listeners on the faith underlying the Wari, PM Modi spoke about the belief of the devotees on how Lord Vitthal safeguarded the interests of the poor and the deprived to alleviate their suffering. The Wari that attracts pilgrims from across Maharashtra, Karnataka, Goa, Andhra Pradesh and Telangana draws on the inspirational life stories of saints like Dnyaneshwar, Namdev, Eknath, Ram Dass and Tukaram. In its fight against superstitions, the pilgrimage relies on *Barud* or *Abhang* (a form of devotional poetry) that delivers a message of amity, love and brotherhood. Chanting the mantra of enlightenment, the pilgrimage shows the mirror to society by fighting against blind faith and ensuring old evil traditions are eradicated.

VOCAL FOR LOCAL

Prime Minister Modi's mantra, Vocal for Local, centred on boosting local arts and crafts and sustaining the livelihoods of local artisans, has been amplified through *Mann Ki Baat*. Festivals from Raksha Bandhan to Diwali are putting the spotlight on local products to keep the consumption economy going alongside sustainable livelihoods:

> Festivals lend a sweetness to our relationships, bring a warmth of togetherness in the family and foster brotherhood in society. They connect the individual with society. It is a natural journey from the self to the collective. And the 'I' gets an opportunity to transform into a 'We'. As far as the economy is concerned, hundreds of families start making Rakhis in small household units, many months before the festival of Rakhi. A variety of Rakhis are made in a whole range of materials, from khadi to silken threads. People prefer homemade Rakhis these days. Rakhi makers and their sellers, sweets shops vendors—the professions of hundreds, thousands flourish on the occasion of a festival. The households of our poor brethren and their families are dependent in a way on these activities. When we light a 'diya', an earthen lamp on Deepawali, it is not merely a festival of lights, a festival that illuminates the entire house; it is directly connected with those poor families who make small 'diyas' or earthen lamps.[12]

The intricately woven annual seasonal cycle of festivals and fairs across India, not only keeps the wheels of the local economy

---

[12]'PM's "Mann ki Baat" Programme on All India Radio', *PMIndia*, 30 July 2017, https://tinyurl.com/muxh8u77. Accessed on 7 April 2023.

spinning but also ensures communities remain vibrant throughout the year. Dwelling at length on the vibrancy of Krishna Janma Mahotsav, the festival of the birth of Lord Krishna celebrated throughout India, PM Modi spoke on the infusion of energy within the youth through this festival. He spoke on the greatness of Lord Krishna's personality and his inspiration in finding solutions to modern-day problems. The PM dwelled on his diverse talents and humane values.

There were times when he would immerse himself in performing the RAAS; at other times he would be in the midst of cows and cowherds; sometimes indulging in sports and games; often playing the flute. A personality brimming with diverse talents and immense capability, yet devoted to empowering society and people, a persona that embodied pioneering accomplishments, a repository, a savior of people. What qualities should the virtue of friendship possess? Who can forget the incident of Sudama? And on the battlefield? Despite his myriad facets of greatness, assuming the role of a charioteer! Or running errands such as lifting a hillock, or at other times picking up leftover leaf plates!

My attention is drawn towards two Mohans. One is the Sudarshan Chakra bearing Mohan and the other is the Charkha bearing Mohan.

The Sudarshan Chakra bearing Mohan left the banks of the Yamuna for the sea beach of Gujarat, establishing himself in the city of Dwarika, while the Mohan born on the sea beach reached the banks of the Yamuna, breathing his last in Delhi. Sudarshan Chakra bearing Mohan, thousands of years ago, had amply used his wisdom, his sense of duty, his might, his worldview to avert war, to prevent conflict, a sign of the times then. And spinning-wheel bearing Mohan too chose a similar path, for the sake of Freedom, for preserving human values, for strengthening the basic elements of personality and character—for this he lent a certain hue to the freedom struggle, a turn, that left the whole world awe struck, which it still remains today. The importance of selfless service, the importance of knowledge, or be it marching ahead smilingly, amidst the trials and tribulations of life, we can learn all these from Lord Krishna's life's message. And that is why Shri Krishna is known as Jagatguru—teacher to the world… 'Krishnam Vande Jagadgurum'.[13]

Just as Lord Krishna's message has a global appeal, our festivals also convey a universal message that promotes the well-being of the entire planet. The PM highlighted how the festival of Diwali was no longer confined to India's borders. With many governments and parliaments across the world joining in Diwali festivities, the universal message of India's centuries-old festival has many brand ambassadors. With the US postal service releasing a special postage stamp, the PMs of the United Kindgom (UK) and Canada joining in the festivities, Singapore marking a special observation and Australia and New Zealand celebrating the festival of lights, Diwali has emerged as a festival for the entire planet to move from darkness to light.[14]

A lesser-known festival of lights was no less inspiring to *Mann Ki Baat* listeners both in India and across the world, with the Sikh diaspora observing Guru Nanak's birth.

---

[13]"PM's Address in 3rd Episode of "Mann Ki Baat 2.0', *PMIndia*, 25 August 2019, https://tinyurl.com/yckp5ycj. Accessed on 6 April 2023.

[14]"Diwali stamp released by US Postal Service', *The Economic Times*, 6 October 2016, https://tinyurl.com/uzz5x36w. Accessed on 13 April 2023.

My dear countrymen, during Diwali festivities, Kartik Purnima is also a festival of lights called Prakash Utsav. Guru Nanak Dev, his teachings and blessings are very relevant even now and are a source of inspiration for humanity as a whole. Service, truth and everybody's well-being was the message of Guru Nanak Dev. Peace, unity and harmony were his principal teachings. Every teaching of Guru Nanak Dev preached that a campaign should be carried on to abolish superstitions, social disparities and social evils from the society. It was then an era when evils such as untouchability, casteism and the chasm between the rich and the poor were at their peak. Guru Nanak Dev picked Bhai Laalo, as his co-worker at that crucial juncture. Let us also follow the light of knowledge bestowed upon us by Guru Nanak Dev which inspires us to end social disparities, exhorts us to do our bit to fight against the evil of disparity. In our march to achieve 'Sab Ka Saath, Sab Ka Vikas', Co-operation from ALL, Development of ALL, we cannot have a better guiding force than Guru Nanak Dev.[15]

---

[15]'PM's "Mann Ki Baat" Programme on All India Radio on 30 October 2016', *PMIndia,* 30 October 2016, https://tinyurl.com/bde7s8u6. Accessed on 7 April 2023.

CHAPTER 10

AN ODE TO ICONS AND HEROES

If there was an alternative framing for *Mann Ki Baat*, it would perhaps have been *Jan ki Baat* or conversations of the common Indian. As *Mann Ki Baat* approaches its hundredth-episode milestone, several hundred citizens making a difference within their communities and impacting society at large have found mentions of their exemplary grassroots efforts in the journey of the programme. Every episode had several of these unsung citizens and their efforts at its heart, with some of them even conversing with PM Narendra Modi and sharing their experiences over airwaves.

These agents of change at the grassroots instilled confidence that India was transforming. Additionally, numerous icons across India's history, spanning centuries, were highlighted on *Mann Ki Baat*, serving as role models to learn from and follow. While Gandhi and Ambedkar have been the two most cited icons on *Mann Ki Baat*, the list is long and diverse. Swami Vivekananda was one of the very first of iconic Indians to feature on the programme. Sharing the parable of the lioness and her cub that was often mentioned by Swami Vivekananda, PM Modi set the tone for what is now a nine-year saga of awakening the souls of his fellow citizens.

> My countrymen, 1.25 crore Indians have infinite strength and capabilities. We need to understand ourselves. We need to identify our inner strengths and like Swami Ji always used to say, we need to carry our self-respect, identify ourselves and move forward in life and be successful, which in turn, make our nation a winning and successful country [sic]. I believe, all our countrymen with a population of 1.25 crores are efficient, strong and can stand against any odds with confidence.[1]

Tracing historical connections between iconic personalities, their works of literature and the inspirations for those works, PM Modi has bridged the artificially created political divides of regionalism to underscore India's cultural unity. A glimpse of this was revealed in October 2017 when he spoke at length about Bhagini Nivedita or Sister Nivedita, an Irish-origin disciple of Swami Vivekananda who made India her home. Marking her 150th birth anniversary, he recalled the Tamil poem dedicated to her called, 'Pudhumai Penn' (New Woman), written by another icon of India, Subramania Bharati, who was known for his nationalism and patriotic poetry. Recalling this Tamil poem dedicated to the issue of women empowerment, PM Modi revealed how Bhagini Nivedita was an inspiration for Bharati.

In the same breath, making yet another connection between spirituality and science, he also shared her efforts to help Jagadish

---

[1]'English Rendering of Text of PM's First Mann Ki Baat to the Nation on Radio', *PMIndia*, 3 October 2014, https://tinyurl.com/2cks9k9z. Accessed on 6 April 2023.

Chandra Bose, the renowned Indian scientist who went on to lay the foundations of modern Indian science through the Bose Institute.

> Bhagini Nivedita ji also helped the great scientist Jagdish Chandra Bose. She helped publication of Bose's research and publicity through her articles and conferences. This is India's unique beauty that spirituality and science complement each other in our culture. Sister Nivedita and Scientist Jagdish Chandra Bose are a powerful testimony to this.[2]

THE VOICES OF SWARAJ

Mann Ki Baat has also been at the forefront of celebrating unsung heroes of India's freedom struggle, the makers of independent India. Urging listeners to draw inspiration from the life stories of these heroes, PM Modi took to airwaves in August 2022 to talk of *Swaraj*, the Doordarshan serial.

> Just a few days ago, I got an opportunity to attend a program of Ministry of Information and Broadcasting, Government of India. There, they had organised the screening of 'Swaraj', the Doordarshan serial. I got an opportunity to attend its premiere. This is a great initiative to acquaint the younger generation of the country with the efforts of unsung heroes and heroines who took part in the freedom movement. It is telecast every Sunday at 9 pm on Doordarshan. And I was told that is going to continue for 75 weeks. I urge you

---

[2]'PM's Mann Ki Baat Programme on All India Radio', *PMIndia*, 29 October 2017, https://tinyurl.com/4cpj4hrn. Accessed on 6 April 2023.

to take time out to watch it yourself and do show it to the children of the house.[3]

Over the course of several episodes, the younger generation of the country was also made familiar with the inspirational life story of tribal icons like Birsa Munda, in addition to the diverse tribal cultures of India and their historical significance. Dedicating 15 November to Janjatiya Gaurav Divas to commemorate tribal pride, PM Modi celebrated the birth anniversary of Bhagwan Birsa Munda by recalling his innately tribal ethics of sustainable living and conservation.

> Friends, when it comes to Dharti Aba Birsa Munda, let's look at his short life span; even today we can learn a lot from him and Dharti Aba had said—'This earth is ours, we are its protectors.' There is also a sense of duty for the motherland in this sentence and there is also a feeling of our duty for the environment. He had always emphasized that we should not forget our tribal culture, we should not go far from it at all. Even today, we can learn a lot about nature and environment from the tribal societies of the country.[4]

Another unsung hero from Meghalaya has been the subject of *Mann Ki Baat*. Speaking about U Tirot Sing Syiem on his death anniversary, PM Modi recalled how he fiercely opposed the British conspiracy to control the Khasi Hills and destroy the culture there.

Making little-known connections across the life journeys of iconic personalities to create contemporary lessons, the PM

---

[3]"PM's Address in the 92nd Episode of "Mann Ki Baat"', *PMIndia*, 28 August 2022, https://tinyurl.com/5dmjsv2w. Accessed on 6 April 2023.
[4]"PM's Address in the 94th Episode of "Mann Ki Baat"', *PMIndia*, 30 October 2022, https://tinyurl.com/4m4nysre. Accessed on 13 April 2023.

reminded his listeners of how eternal vigilance is the price of freedom, whether you are a revolutionary or a poet laureate:

It is a matter of great pride for all of us that Rabindranath Tagore and his memories are a shared heritage. The National Anthem of Bangladesh too, has been composed by Gurudev Rabindranath Tagore. There is a very interesting fact about Gurudev that in 1913 he was not only the first Asian to receive the Nobel Prize, but Knighthood was also conferred upon him by the British. After the Jallianwala massacre, by the British in 1919, Rabindranath Tagore was one of the legendary figures, who raised their voices in protest. And it was at the same time, that this event left a very deep impact on a twelve-year-old boy. The inhuman massacre at Jallianwala Bagh, provided a new inspiration and mission in life to that young teenager, who until then had spent his days playing merrily in his fields. And Bhagat, that 12-year-old boy in 1919, evolved to be the martyr Bhagat Singh, our dear hero and inspiration. On the 23rd of March, Bhagat Singh Ji and his comrades, Sukhdev and Rajguru, were hanged to death by the British, and we are all aware of that. There was a sense of fulfilment on the faces of Bhagat Singh, Sukhdev and Rajguru for having served Mother India—there was no fear of death. They had sublimated all their dreams for the freedom of Mother India. These three heroes inspire us to this day. It would be impossible to express in words the story of the supreme sacrifice of Bhagat Singh, Sukhdev and Rajguru. And the entire British Empire feared these three young men. They were in jail, certain to be hanged, but still the British remained anxious about how to deal with them. That is why, though the scheduled date was the 24th, they were hanged on the 23rd of March. This was done clandestinely, which is not the usual practice. And later, their remains were brought to present day Punjab, and were secretly cremated. Many years ago, when I first got the chance to go there, I could feel a certain vibration in that place. And I would certainly urge the youth of our country to go to Punjab, whenever they get the chance, and visit the 'samadhi' of Bhagat Singh, Sukhdev, Rajguru, Bhagat Singh's mother and Batukeshwar Dutt.[5]

Making yet another connection between poets and revolutionaries, the PM revealed rare facets of Veer Savarkar's personality in the May 2018 episode. Marching with poetry and revolution, the sensitive poet and courageous revolutionary Savarkar has been an inspiration of selfless service to the nation and community. He was brutally imprisoned by the British Empire in isolation in the Cellular Jail in Andaman and Nicobar Islands for several years. Describing his personality, PM Modi spoke on his many special qualities both as a worshipper of *shastra* (weapons) and *shaastra* (knowledge). These qualities of Savarkar were the subject of a poem composed by the former PM Atal Bihari Vajpayee. *Mann Ki Baat* listeners were treated to a recitation of this poem when PM Modi took to airwaves to describe Savarkar's many qualities as a poet and as a social reformer.

> Savarkar means brilliance, Savarkar means sacrifice, Savarkar means penance, Savarkar means substance, Savarkar means logic, Savarkar means youth, Savarkar means an arrow, and Savarkar means a Sword! Behold![6]

---

[5]'PM's "Mann ki Baat" Programme on All India Radio', *PMIndia*, 26 March 2017, https://tinyurl.com/ydwh4ewu. Accessed on 6 April 2023.
[6]'PM's "Mann Ki Baat" Programme on All India Radio', *PMIndia*, 27 May 2018, https://tinyurl.com/45mj4p7z. Accessed on 6 April 2023.

Preceding Savarkar by several decades was Bal Gangadhar Tilak, who combined erudition with the revolutionary zeal to challenge colonialism. Narrating an anecdote from 1900s, when Tilak visited Ahmedabad, PM Modi discussed Tilak's influence on Sardar Vallabhbhai Patel, which grew into deep reverence. With Tilak's demise in 1920, Patel, who was then the president of the Municipal Board of Ahmedabad, decided to commemorate a statue for Tilak. He immediately selected Victoria Garden, which was named after the British Queen, as the venue for Tilak's memorial. The British were naturally not happy with this and the collector continually kept denying permission. But Sardar Patel's persistence and his uncompromising stance ensured that the statue got built and unveiled by none other than Mahatma Gandhi on 28 February 1929. During that inaugural ceremony, Gandhi remarked that with Patel's arrival, Ahmedabad Municipal Corporation had not only got its man, but it had got strength, on the basis of which building the statue of Tilak had become possible. Tilak's statue in Ahmedabad is rare for its sitting posture with his famous slogan '*Swaraj hamara janma siddha adhikar hai*' (Swaraj is our birthright) inscribed on the pedestal.

The deep, lasting influence of the revolutionary spirit of our freedom fighters on PM Modi became evident when he dwelt at length on the sacrifices of Chandra Shekhar Azad, who incidentally shared his birthday with Tilak.

After 50 years of Tilak's birth, on the same day i.e. on July 23, another son of Mother India was born, who sacrificed his life so that his countrymen could breathe freely in an atmosphere of freedom. I am talking about none other than Chandra Shekhar Azad. Where will you find a young man in India who will not be inspired listening to these lines—

Sarfaroshi ki tamanna ab hamare dil mein hai
Dekhna hai zor kitna baazu-e-qaatil mein hai
(The desire for martyrdom is now in our hearts
Let us see the strength in the arms of my executioner)

[...] It was my privilege and good fortune that I had the opportunity of going to Chandrasekhar Azad's native village of Alirajpur in Madhya Pradesh. I had the opportunity to pay homage in Chandra Shekhar Azad Park in Allahabad, Chandra Shekhar Azad Ji was a brave man who did not wish to die by the bullet of foreigners—he wished to fight for independence as a free man and if he had to die, he wished to remain a free man! This is what was so special about him.[7]

The underlying spirit of national purpose was reinforced by PM Modi through Pandit Deendayal Upadhyaya's Antyodaya philosophy aimed at uplifting the poorest of the poor. Marking the birth anniversary of this icon, who has been described as one of the greatest Indian thinkers of the twentieth century, PM Modi took to airwaves in September 2021 to explain Upadhyaya's philosophy. The PM Modi explained and emphasized the importance of the economic philosophy of Antyodaya and policies focussed on empowering society in contemporary India. He also highlighted how these ideas have inspired numerous change initiatives championed through *Mann Ki Baat*.

Recalling the life of another veteran associate Nanaji Deshmukh, PM Modi highlighted how both Nanaji and Pandit Deendayal Upadhyaya remained far away from the corridors of power but lived every moment for the people, kept fighting all

---

[7]'PM's Mann Ki Baat Programme on All India Radio', *PMIndia*, 29 July 2018, https://tinyurl.com/2p9dv2a3. Accessed on 6 April 2023.

odds to follow the principle of '*Sarv jan hitay, sarv jan sukhay*' (In the interest of all people, for the good of all people) and endeavoured tirelessly to ensure that this was adopted for the development of communities. Talking about how Nanaji had left politics and dedicated his life to Gramodaya, he made yet another connection between two iconic personalities by sharing India's former president Dr Abdul Kalam's words on Nanaji's contribution in rural development.

> Like Gandhiji, Deen Dayal Upadhyaya ji also talked about the last person at the farthest fringes. Deen Dayalji talked about the poorest of the poor the deprived, distressed ones and spoke of how, through education, employment or otherwise their lives could be transformed. [8]

It was not only icons of a bygone era but also living legends that stood with the PM through this journey.[9] The September 2019 episode of *Mann Ki Baat* was special, as it featured a rare conversation with the Nightingale of India, Bharat Ratna Lata Mangeshkar, whom the PM refers to as 'Didi'. As Mangeshkar had borne witness to the numerous phases and distinct eras of India's developmental journey, the warmth of the conversation on *Mann Ki Baat* and her blessings to PM Modi, conveyed to him in her golden voice, will forever be etched in history.

---

[8]'PM's Mann Ki Baat Programme on All India Radio', *PMIndia*, 24 September 2017, https://tinyurl.com/mryk53rh. Accessed on 6 April 2023.
[9]'Lata Mangeshkar Is "Special Guest" at PM Modi's Mann ki Baat', *Hindustan Times*, 29 September 2019, https://tinyurl.com/nvsbpcav. Accessed on 12 April 2023.

POWER OF NEW INDIA

Beyond these legendary names, several selfless citizens have made their appearance on *Mann Ki Baat* over the last nine years through their efforts and impacts at the grassroots. In many cases, their efforts had been going on for several years prior to their mention on *Mann Ki Baat*. There is, however, a difference between merely chronicling voluntary social work and making a connection to a larger national purpose. Every individual effort inspired and amplified by *Mann Ki Baat* added up to a bigger purpose, like a drop of water contributing to the ocean. From Swachh Bharat to water conservation, coming to the aid of fellow citizens during demonetization or combating the Covid-19 pandemic collectively, individual contributions had a multiplier effect through *Mann Ki Baat*, ensuring their overall success.

The importance of every contribution was reflected in the art work by Akbar Saheb, an artist living in Abu Dhabi who sketched various topics of *Mann Ki Baat*; Ahmed Ali, a rickshaw puller who built nine schools for the underprivileged in Assam; or Saidul Laskar, who built a hospital for the underprivileged in West Bengal.

Thirteen years ago, on account of a delay in medical treatment, a cab driver from Kolkata, Saidul Laskar lost his sister. He vowed to construct a hospital in order to ensure that none of the underprivileged face a similar situation due to lack of medical aid. In this mission of his, Saidul sold off family jewellery and raised funds through charity. His cab passengers too contributed large-heartedly. A young engineer girl donated her first salary for this noble cause. This way, after mobilizing funds for twelve long years, Saidul's mammoth efforts paid rich dividends. Today, through sheer hard work and a firm resolve, a thirty bedded hospital has finally come up at Punri Village near Kolkata. This is the power of New India.[10]

Prime Minister Modi has consistently delivered the message of dreaming big, persisting with the dreams and never being deterred by failures. Quoting one of his favourite icons, Dr Abdul Kalam, PM Modi spoke of how Dr Kalam's failure to become a pilot resulted in India gaining a great scientist and, ultimately, a popular president.

I am reminded of our nation's ex-President, Shri A. P. J. Abdul Kalam. In his book "My Journey-Transforming dreams into Action", he has mentioned an incident that took place in his life. He says that he always aspired to become a pilot. However, when he tried to become a pilot, he failed and could not clear his exams. Now, you can see that his failure gave him a great opportunity in his life. He became a great scientist of our nation. He became the President of India and his contribution stands unparalleled in the field of nuclear energy in India. Therefore, friends, please do not bend yourselves under the burden of failure. Failure is a kind of opportunity. Do not let the failure go without learning a lesson from it. Try to search for a hope and opportunity that lies hidden in your failure. This is my humble request to all my young friends, and also to their family members—if your son fails, please do not create an atmosphere which can force him to lose all hopes in his life. Sometimes, the children's failure is associated with their

---

[10]'PM's Mann Ki Baat Programme on All India Radio', *PMIndia*, 25 March 2018, https://tinyurl.com/2u2rjdz7. Accessed on 6 April 2023.

parents' dream which leads to various problems in future. It should not happen. Fighting with failures can provide us the strength to live our lives peacefully.[11]

Dr Abdul Kalam's mantra was shared through *Mann Ki Baat* to a national audience and surely had an impact over the years, with so many unsung citizens going beyond the demands of everyday life to make a difference to their communities.

The nation was witness to the efforts of a sarpanch in a remote village of Haryana gain global recognition when his #SelfieWithDaughter hashtag went viral, thanks to *Mann Ki Baat*. Sunil Jaglan's innovative idea to boost the government's initiative, Beti Bachao Beti Padhao (that first gained national attention on *Mann Ki Baat* in 2015), has since bubbled up into a movement of sorts. With period charts to battle menstrual taboos in rural Haryana, Jaglan's grassroots efforts to empower the girl child have demonstrated how *Mann Ki Baat* themes have taken a life of their own beyond airwaves to bring about societal change.

Jatin Lalit Singh from Bansa Village of Hardoi district in Uttar Pradesh and Sanjay Kashyap in Jharkhand stand out for their efforts to popularize reading, targeting rural students and underprivileged students through community libraries. While Jatin Lalit Singh's community centre boasts of more than 3,000 books, roping in 40 volunteers, Sanjay Kashyap's library movement spans multiple districts in Jharkhand. Book reading was the subject of the last *Mann Ki Baat* episode of 2021 that put the spotlight on a retired principal, Dr Kurella Vittalacharya, who had converted his residence in Yellanki village of Ramannapet block in Yadadri

---

[11]'English Rendering of the Text of Prime Minister Shri Narendra Modi's Address to the Nation on All India Radio', *PMIndia*, 31 May 2015, https://tinyurl.com/3afhytvn. Accessed on 6 April 2023.

Bhuvanagiri into a library for the public with more than 2 lakh books. His efforts have inspired a similar library movement in eight other villages in the Nalgonda District of Telangana.

Jamuna Mani Singh is an Accredited Social Health Activist (ASHA) from Odisha, whose work in combating malaria found mention on *Mann Ki Baat* in November 2015. ASHA is a nationwide collective of health activists working in their local communities to promote public health awareness. Hailing from a small village, Tenda Gaon, in Balasore district, with a predominantly tribal population, Jamuna decided that she will not let anyone die of malaria. She would be the first one to reach if there was news of fever in any household. She would put to use the primary training she received and give treatment accordingly. She would reach out to every household to disseminate information about using mosquito repellents and nets. Her fight against malaria was recognized duly by the Odisha government.

Emphasizing the ethic of giving back to the community and paying back the debt of society, PM Modi highlighted several instances of community service by Anganwadi workers, women's SHGs and countless other citizens. One such effort was One Teacher, One Call, championed by Deepmala Pandey, the principal of a school in Dabhora Gangapur in Uttar Pradesh's Bareilly district. She, along with 350 teachers, would go from village to village calling for children with disabilties, looking out for them and then ensuring their admission in one school or the other, so that they were not disadvantaged during Covid-19.

Noting many such instances of selfless service to the community during the nationwide lockdown in response to Covid-19, PM Modi gave a national shout-out to everyday heroes who stepped up to the aid of their fellow citizens. Gautam Das, a hand-cart puller who lived on daily wages in Agartala, fed the needy from his earnings, while Balbir Kaur, a sarpanch in Jammu, set up a 30-bed quarantine centre. From mask-making to sanitization products, PM Modi recounted citizens' contributions, big and small, in combating the pandemic.

In recognition of the fact that combating climate change is everyone's concern and responsibility, PM Modi highlighted the grassroots efforts of Noor Jehan towards conservation and sustainable living. Noor Jehan, whose name means the light of the world, is spreading light to homes of the poor in a remote corner of Kanpur, thus taking small steps towards sustainable living. Noor Jehan had formed a *samiti* (committee) of women who manufacture lanterns that run on solar energy. They rent the lantern for ₹100 per month. People take the lanterns in the evening and return them in the morning for recharging. At an expense of ₹3–4 per day, the entire house is illuminated. Noor Jehan works the entire day to recharge the lanterns in the solar energy plant so that she can service around 500 households.

Sharing the spotlight with Noor Jehan is Rajappan from Naduvilakkara in Kerala. Sharing his story in his own words, he says:

> I am a differently abled man known for collecting plastic and other waste from canals, river and backwaters. I always have Prime Minister's words in my mind, they are an inspiration. My ambition is to maintain clean surroundings and water bodies. The community has empowered me further thanks to Mann Ki Baat recognising my efforts.[12]

From preserving nature to culture, *Mann Ki Baat* has featured the likes of Sikari Tissau, who has toiled hard to preserve the

---

[12]As told to Doordarshan in March 2023.

culture of the Northeast. A resident of the Karbi Anglong district of Assam, he has been documenting the Karbi language for the last 20 years. Karbi, the language of the tribal community there, has been fast disappearing from the mainstream. Through Tissau's efforts, significant information about the Karbi language has been documented, ensuring its preservation for future generations. With his efforts finding a mention on *Mann Ki Baat*, Tissau has since taken on the onerous task of editing a multilingual dictionary of tribal languages of the Northeast, comprising Assamese, Bodo, Deori, Garo, Mising, Rabha, Tiwa and English.

Adopting storytelling as a means to preserve and propagate native wisdom from India's myriad languages and dialects, is the website *Gaathastory.in*, run by Amar Vyas and his colleagues. At the peak of Covid-19, PM Modi brought to the attention of his listeners many such endeavours that were popularizing stories from rural India, giving the instance of Vaishali Vyawahare Deshpande, who was popularizing storytelling in Marathi. Websites like *Kathalaya. org* and the Indian Story Telling Network did commendable work; so did the Bengaluru Storytelling Society. Highlighting the significance of storytelling, PM Modi encouraged storytellers to engage the new generation of India by sharing stories about the lives of remarkable men and women.

Sometimes, the initiatives of these heroes even crossed borders and oceans to put the spotlight on little-known efforts back home. Team India—Vision for Tribals made news in India in August 2015 when PM Modi highlighted the efforts of Dr Hitendra Mahajan and Dr Mahendra Mahajan, siblings from Nashik, Maharashtra. The brothers had won a 4,800 km cycle race in the US, bringing attention to the cause of the tribal population of India.

The PM has made it a point to bring out the struggles of such heroes and their impact over the past nine years. Of particular note is how, during his premiership, the state awards have been fundamentally transformed from rewarding the elite to recognizing common citizens making an impact at the grassroots of society. Popularizing the award with the catchphrase 'People's Padma', *Mann Ki Baat* brought to the fore little-known aspects of the life struggles of the many winners over the past few years. Expressing pride over Indian citizens being nominated for People's Padma awards without any recommendations, PM Modi told his listeners how, in the past, there was a certain methodology of awarding these awards every year, and how his government has strived to change the process. Listeners were told how the identity of the awardee was no longer the deciding factor of the award; rather, the importance of their work and its impact was the new deciding factor. Further, any citizen could nominate any person in the country. This, according to PM Modi, brought out yet another aspect of how the Indian democracy had gone digital to bring transparency to the entire nomination process.

Recognizing the importance of role models, the PM has put national spotlight on both unsung heroes and forgotten icons across India to constantly guide, motivate and inspire his listeners. In the process, his dialogue with India has shattered glass ceilings and social barriers. Prime Minister Modi has stimulated social change by leveraging the network effect, leading to an increasing number of change advocates emerging from every corner of India's diverse towns, villages and communities.

CHAPTER 11

HARD AND SOFT POWER

Prime Minister Modi's global outreach through *Mann Ki Baat* is a case study in soft diplomacy in the age of the Internet. It is also without a parallel in recent times, for there is no precedent of a head of government sharing a domestic mass outreach platform with a visiting head of State to engage in a multifaceted public dialogue. This global moment came quite early on for *Mann Ki Baat*, when, in its fourth episode, then President of the US Barack Obama visited India to be the chief guest at the Republic Day Parade. The *Mann Ki Baat* episode that aired on 27 January 2015 broke from its usual format with a joint recording between PM Modi and President Obama taking questions from listeners across India. The free-wheeling conversation between the two leaders spanned multiple topics, from the girl child to public health, from engaging global youth to drawing inspiration from historical personalities. Perhaps most interesting of these were the personal life stories of both leaders and their parallel journeys to the highest public offices in their respective nations.

Riding on this high note, *Mann Ki Baat* has seen its global engagement straddle a wide range of subjects, most prominent of which has been yoga. Starting with the first International Yoga Day in 2015, PM Modi has creatively leveraged *Mann Ki Baat* to both put the spotlight on global support for the International Yoga Day, as well as on individual champions of yoga across the planet.

> Take 'Japan Yoga Niketan', which has made Yoga popular throughout Japan. Japan Yoga Niketan runs many institutes and conducts various training courses. Italy's Ms. Antonietta Rozzi, has started 'Sarv Yoga International', and popularized Yoga throughout Europe. These are inspirational examples in themselves.[1]

The Internet has lowered barriers significantly for the flow of ideas across borders. The popularity of yoga owes as much to its intrinsic appeal for a healthy lifestyle as to globalization of information. A tweet by PM Modi of a photo of a Vietnamese child doing yoga garnered worldwide attention. It is this spirit of global connectivity that *Mann Ki Baat* has embodied in championing yoga bringing together men and women, old and young, across villages and cities from both developed and developing countries:

> Yoga in true terms, became the core reason to connect the entire world. I do not know how the intellectual class; elites of the world would analyze this event. But I can feel and every Indian can experience that the whole world is very

---

[1]'PM's Address in "Mann Ki Baat 2.0" Programme on All India Radio', *PMIndia*, 30 June 2019, https://tinyurl.com/3hhx3ecs. Accessed on 10 April 2023.

curious to know more about India. The world wants to know about the values, the rituals and the heritage of India. It is our responsibility that without any artificiality we share our legacy and introduce ourselves to the world. We can only do this when we ourselves are proud of our traditions.[2]

The world's curiosity about India has found a steady companion in *Mann Ki Baat*, evoking interest, posing questions, exploring answers and, above all, narrating experiences. In enabling this outreach, PM Modi has forged familial bonds with societies and peoples across the planet, finding common causes and seeking shared experiences. A fine example of this is South Africa, with both Gandhi and Mandela as twin symbols of a historical bond that was further amplified by *Mann Ki Baat*. Bangladesh's path to independence and its long-standing friendship with India manifested in a joint radio station that found its echo on *Mann Ki Baat*. Akashvani Maitree, launched in 2016 as a joint radio service of All India Radio (AIR) and Bangladesh Betar, has become a platform for cultural exchange as envisioned by PM Modi.

Indian cultural ambassadors across the world have found recognition back in India for their varied efforts, with *Mann Ki Baat* chronicling them in detail. Greek singer Konstantinos Kalaitzis's rendering of 'Vaishnav Jan To' and his photo-book on Indian music got nationwide attention, while Japanese art director Hiroshi Koike's Mahabharata project reminded listeners of the wide footprint of Indian art and culture in Southeast Asia.

---

[2]'English Rendering of Prime Minister's "Mann ki Baat" Address on All India Radio', *PMIndia*, 28 June 2015, https://tinyurl.com/mrydct8a. Accessed on 10 April 2023.

This project was started in Cambodia and it is continuing for the last 9 years. Hiroshi Koike ji performs every task in a very different way. Every year, he travels to one country in Asia and produces parts of the Mahabharata with local artists and musicians there. Through this project, he has done productions and given stage performances in nine countries including India, Cambodia and Indonesia. Hiroshi Koike-ji brings together artists who have had a diverse background in classical and traditional Asian performing art. Because of that, different hues are seen in his work. Performers from Indonesia, Thailand, Malaysia and Japan make it more attractive through Java dance, Balinese dance, Thai dance. The special thing is that in this each performer speaks in his own mother tongue and the choreography very beautifully displays this diversity and the diversity of music makes this production more lively. Their aim is to bring to the fore the importance of diversity and co-existence in our society and what peace should really be like.[3]

In the same episode, PM Modi also paid rich tributes to Yugo Sako for his Ramayana production in Japanese during the 1980s, and mentioned how the animated masterpiece is acquiring a new avatar in 4K, thanks to the efforts of Atsushi Matsuo and Kenji Yoshi of the TEM Production Company.

The soft power reach of Indian music from Guyana in the Caribbean to Tanzania in Africa has created awareness of artistes and Indian origin art forms through *Mann Ki Baat*. Sedu Dembele of Mali may not be of Indian origin, but he is no

---

[3]"PM's Address in the 89th Episode of "Mann Ki Baat"", *PMIndia*, 29 May 2022, https://tinyurl.com/p2fuxceh. Accessed on 10 April 2023.

less an ambassador for Bollywood and all things Indian with his radio show that found an echo on *Mann Ki Baat.* Sedu, who is a teacher in a public school in Kita, a town in Mali, impressed PM Modi with his radio show in French that is dedicated to Bollywood music and airs on Saturdays. Sedu's love for Indian films has also manifested in another two-hour programme at 9.00 p.m. every Sunday, in which he narrates the story of an entire Bollywood film in French and in Bambara, the native tongue of Mali.

Mann Ki Baat traces the popularity of Indian culture from Africa to Latin America and across geographies by sharing the stellar role being played by people like the nonagenarian Professor Aida Albrecht and her Hastinapur Foundation. With 40,000 members and over 30 branches across Argentina for the propagation of Vedic traditions, the foundation has published more than 100 Vedic and philosophical texts in Spanish. No less inspiring is the endeavour of Jonas Masetti, on the other side of the Amazon, who teaches Vedanta and the Bhagavad Gita in Brazil. Running an institution called Vishwavidya situated in the hills of Petrópolis (at an hour's distance from Rio de Janeiro), Jonas had earlier studied Vedanta philosophy in India, staying at Arsha Vidya Gurukulam in Coimbatore for four years. Using technology to propagate his message, Jonas, through a daily podcast and other efforts over the last seven years, has taught over one lakh students. The conversation with American-born Jadurani Dasi on how Indian culture has found a home across the oceans through movements like the International Society for Krishna Consciousness (ISKCON) was also truly inspiring.

THE HEALING POWER OF AYURVEDA

One of the most interesting anecdotes shared by PM Modi was on Ayurvedic tourism in Kerala and the manner in which it aided Rosemary Odinga, daughter of former Kenyan PM Raila Odinga.

Friends, a few days ago I had a meeting with my friend and former Prime Minister of Kenya, Raila Odinga. This meeting was interesting but also very emotional. Since we are very good friends, we also discuss freely. While both of us were in a conversation, Odinga ji told [me] about his daughter. His daughter Rosemary had a brain tumour and because of this she had to undergo surgery. However, one side-effect of this was that Rosemary almost lost her eyesight; she stopped seeing. You can imagine what must have happened to the daughter... and we can also guess the condition of the father, we can understand his feelings. In hospitals all over the world...there was not any major country in the world, where he had not tried his best for the treatment of his daughter. He searched the big countries of the world, but, there was no success and in a way, giving up all hopes, there was an atmosphere of despair in the entire household. Meanwhile, someone suggested [to] him to come to India for Ayurveda treatment and even though he had tried a lot and was tired, yet he thought that let's try once again...see what happens! He came to India, started getting his daughter treated at an Ayurvedic hospital in Kerala. The daughter stayed here for a long time. The effect of this Ayurvedic treatment was such that Rosemary's eyesight returned to a great extent. You can imagine, as if a new lease of life was given and light came back into Rosemary's life. As the new light has come in the whole family, Odinga ji was so emotional while telling me this and that he wishes, that the knowledge and science of Ayurveda of India, should be brought to Kenya. The type of plants that are used in it will be cultivated by them and he will do his best to get more people to benefit from it.[4]

Further elaborating on the experience of Rosemary Odinga in availing Ayurvedic treatment in India, *Nation*, a Kenyan newspaper, carried a detailed report by Leon Lidigu, a health reporter with the Nation Media Group. The report quoted Rosemary saying that after two years of treatment, she was able to even read messages on her phone with her vision substantially improved. The report also quoted Raila Odinga making a rare political promise to bring Ayurveda to Kenya with the support of PM Modi.[5]

KHADI'S SOFT POWER

Not just Kenya, but the whole of Africa has been at the centre of India's soft power with the Pravasi Bharatiya Divas, the annual Government of India celebration of the Indian diaspora, drawing its origins from the date fixed to mark the return of emigrant Mohandas Karamchand Gandhi back to India from distant South Africa. Gandhi was as much an inspiration to independent India as he is a symbol for the Indian diaspora scattered across the globe for having lived the immigrant experience and endured its hardships.

Gandhi's global popularity has also inspired the third prong of India's soft power projection apart from yoga and AYUSH—

---

[4]"PM's Address in the 86th Episode of "Mann Ki Baat"", *PMIndia*, 27 February 2022, *PMIndia*, https://tinyurl.com/49atpuby. Accessed on 10 April 2023.
[5]Lidigu, Leon, 'Why Raila Turned to Indian Traditional Treatment to Save Daughter's Eyesight', *Nation*, 25 February 2022, https://tinyurl.com/2p93wenm. Accessed on 10 April 2023.

khadi. Recalling how a khadi handkerchief gifted by Gandhi was treasured by (late) Queen Elizabeth II of Britain, PM Modi gave a glimpse into khadi's soft power.

> During my past UK visit, in London, the Queen of Britain, Queen Elizabeth had invited me to dine with her. The atmosphere was imbued with maternal warmth, and I was served with great affection. Afterwards when she showed me a small thread-spun khadi handkerchief, her eyes lit up. With great respect and in an emotion filled voice, she said, that Mahatma Gandhi had sent this handkerchief to her as a wedding gift. So many years have passed and yet, Queen Elizabeth has treasured the handkerchief gifted by Mahatma Gandhi. And she was happy to show it to me, when I went there. As I gazed at it, the Queen encouraged me to touch it. A small gift by Mahatma Gandhi, has become a part of her life and a part of history.[6]

It does not come as a surprise that Gandhi's championing of khadi continues to inspire and motivate across continents, even several decades after the freedom movement and the call for swadeshi.

> Not only is the popularity of khadi rising it is also being produced in many places of the world. There is a place in Mexico called Oaxaca, there are many villages in this area where the local villagers weave khadi. Today the khadi of this place has gained popularity by the name Oaxaca khadi. How khadi reached Oaxaca is no less interesting. In fact, a young person of Oaxaca, Mark Brown once watched a movie

---

[6]"PM's "Mann Ki Baat" Programme on All India Radio', *PMIndia*, 25 June 2017, https://tinyurl.com/3yebk7zd. Accessed on 10 April 2023.

on Mahatma Gandhi. Brown got so inspired by watching this movie on Bapu that he visited Bapu's ashram in India, understood him and learnt about him in depth. It was then, that Brown realised that khadi was not just a cloth; it was a complete way of life. Brown was deeply moved by the way khadi was intertwined with the rural economy and self-sufficiency. It was here that Brown resolved to work on khadi on his return to Mexico. He introduced the villagers of Oaxaca in Mexico to khadi and trained them. And now Oaxaca khadi has become a brand. The website of this project bears the inscription 'the symbol of Dharma in motion'. You can also find a very interesting interview of Marc Brown on this website. He narrates that initially the people were wary of khadi but ultimately, they got interested and a market got ready for it. He states that these are matters related to Ram Rajya, when you fulfil the needs of the people, the people start connecting with you.[7]

DIASPORA DIPLOMACY

Mann Ki Baat has also celebrated the success of the Indian diaspora at every step of the way, from recognizing the participation of public officials of Indian origin in the Pravasi Bharatiya Divas to drawing attention to the celebration of Indian origin achievers by the European Union in the form of a calendar.

Newly elected MP in New Zealand Dr. Gaurav Sharma took the Oath of office in one of the ancient languages of the

---

[7]'PM's Address in the 17th Episode of "Mann Ki Baat 2.0"', *PMIndia*, 25 October 2020, https://tinyurl.com/3fn9muw9. Accessed on 10 April 2023.

world—Sanskrit. The dissemination of Indian culture on part of an Indian fills us with pride. Through the medium of Mann Ki Baat, I extend best wishes to Gaurav Sharma ji. All of us wish he attains newer achievements in the service of the people of New Zealand.[8]

The popularity of indigenous sports within the diaspora has reached record-setting levels thanks to the inspiration from *Mann Ki Baat* and the constant motivation from PM Modi. In October 2020, *Mann Ki Baat* noted the role of the diaspora in popularizing the indigenous sports of India and dedicated substantial time to discuss Mallakhamb going global. Delving into what spurred Chinmay Patankar and Pradnya Patankar to teach Mallakhamb out of their home in the US, in November 2020, *The Better India* narrated how a backyard in Edison, New Jersey, became the perfect setting for this traditional Indian sport.[9] From forming a federation in the US to demonstrating Mallakhamb at the UN, the Patankars' commitment to popularizing Indian sport exemplifies how the Indian diaspora has emerged as effective brand ambassadors for Indian culture and traditions.

The performance of Kalaripayattu, the traditional martial art of Kerala, by a record number of people, ranging from four-year-old children to 60-year-old senior citizens, at an event organized by the Kalari Club, Dubai together with Dubai Police on the UAE National Day set a world record.

---

[8]"PM's Address in the 18th Episode of "Mann Ki Baat 2.0"", *PMIndia*, 29 November 2020, https://tinyurl.com/29kx98bt. Accessed on 10 April 2023.
[9]Nitnaware, Himanshu, 'Pune to New York to Poland: NRI Takes India's Ancient Mallakhamb to the World', *The Better India*, 24 November 2020, https://tinyurl.com/jc3eet42. Accessed on 19 April 2023.

From martial arts to the Buddha, *Mann Ki Baat* has connected cultural dots across the diaspora and along India's immediate neighbourhood to deepen bonds and impact appreciation of India and its culture. The Buddhist Tourism Circuit is one such initiative that found mention on *Mann Ki Baat*, wherein the programme recalled the ancient Buddhist legacy that saw diffusion of ideas beyond borders:

> It forges a link between us and many Asian countries like China, Japan, Korea, Thailand, Cambodia, and Myanmar where Buddhist traditions and his [sic] preaching are a part of their origins. And this is the very reason that we are developing infrastructure for Buddhist tourism, which is going to connect Southeast Asia with the important Buddhist sites of India. I am also very pleased that the Government of India is a partner in the restoration of many Buddhist temples which also includes the centuries old magnificent Ananda Temple in Bagan in Myanmar. Today, when there is confrontation and human suffering prevalent everywhere in the world, Lord Buddha's teachings show the way to rid hatred from the world with compassion.[10]

Compassion in the face of adversities takes many forms. With disasters in the neighbourhood no longer a distant news story, *Mann Ki Baat* has chronicled how a neighbour's crisis is as much a crisis within the family. Extolling the rescue efforts of the Indian Navy, coming to the aid of neighbouring countries during cyclones, *Mann Ki Baat* has shown how India has harnessed its hard power with compassion across the oceans,

---

[10]'PM's Mann Ki Baat Programme on All India Radio', *PMIndia*, 29 April 2018, https://tinyurl.com/244jsfyh. Accessed on 10 April 2023.

from delivering medical supplies to Fiji to bringing flood relief to Sri Lanka. The programme has also been a vehicle for reinforcing the sentiment that a crisis for one is a crisis for all within the neighbourhood through initiatives like the Bay of Bengal Initiative for Multi-Sectoral Technical and Economic Cooperation (BIMSTEC). India's men and women in uniform have gone far beyond the neighbourhood to not just provide relief but also ensure peace in conflict zones and collaborate on issues of poverty and public health confronting humanity. From vaccines to digital public goods, if India is able to come to the aid of the neighbourhood and beyond today, it is because of PM Modi's push towards *atmanirbharta* or self-reliance.

During an era when globalization was challenged by a once-in-a-hundred-years pandemic and techno-nationalism has come to define geopolitics, *Mann Ki Baat* offers a kaleidoscope to view PM Modi's artful blending of the soft power reach of Indian culture with the hard-nosed realism to build India's economic strength and resilience.

CHAPTER 12

FROM CRADLE TO COMMUNITIES

It would not be an exaggeration to state that no other mass outreach programme has constantly strived to both develop a sense of community and ensure inclusion of all in community initiatives, as has been the case with *Mann Ki Baat*. Two outstanding focal points of inclusion within the programme have been gender and disability. On both of these focal points, PM Modi's outreach is unlike any past precedent in its innately Indian formulation of slogans, monikers and mass messaging.

The consistency that these messages have found a place in *Mann Ki Baat* is a glimpse of how he has viewed community ownership as the fulcrum for mass societal change. With an early focus on it, PM Modi has used *Mann Ki Baat* to converse with children as much as with senior citizens. *Mann Ki Baat* has played a leading role in promoting community engagement, with diverse sections of society contributing to various areas, encompassing inclusion and conservation efforts.

A central theme of the PM's thrust for gender inclusion has been on protecting and educating the girl child. His initiatives to ensure the safety and security of girls in the country, mentioned in his speeches from the ramparts of Red Fort to the studios of the AIR, have broken many taboos in conservative Indian society.

The heartbreaking issue of gender-based violence in India impelled the PM to ask families difficult questions on the conduct of male children during their formative years. His call for the need to create an environment of safety and security for women has spurred a nationwide stand against gender-based violence. He noted that it was the responsibility of society to ensure that girls and women were safe and respected and that perpetrators of gender-based violence are brought to justice.

Mann Ki Baat recognizes the immense potential of empowering the girl child as key to national progress and prosperity, and consistently emphasizes the twin goals of education and empowerment. Dwelling on the importance of educating girls, PM Modi viewed educated and empowered girls as the most powerful agents of change in Indian society.

He has often highlighted the importance of the Beti Bachao Beti Padhao initiative launched in 2015. Terming this initiative as a campaign that seeks to ensure the survival and education of the girl child, PM Modi called for India's daughters to get the same opportunities and necessary resources as its sons, so as to pursue their dreams and aspirations. *Mann Ki Baat* has documented several instances of women led SHGs and female entrepreneurs emerging as job creators and agents of change, thereby highlighting the importance of providing vocational training to girls, so that they become financially independent and contribute to the economy.

Prime Minister Narendra Modi's messages on the issue of female education in India have found an echo beyond banners and pamphlets. They have inspired street art and the uniquely

Indian phenomenon of art on the back of trucks. A direct impact of this these messages has been observed on the number of girls enrolled in primary education, which has increased significantly in the last few years. The increase in the number of girls enrolled in schools of over 2 crore during a three-year period has been a testament to the impact of *Mann Ki Baat* in raising awareness and bringing about social change.

Mann Ki Baat has played a critical role in raising awareness of the importance of nutrition for pregnant women and young children and how nutrition can help reduce the mortality rate of children under the age of five. It has also encouraged community steps to combat malnutrition. The focus on POSHAN Abhiyaan, a flagship programme by the government to combat malnutrition in India, effectively connected the issues of gender inclusion, support for the girl child and combating malnutrition. It aims to do so by bringing together various ministries and stakeholders. It seeks to reduce stunting and under-nutrition among children under five years and also reduce anaemia among all women and adolescents.

Terming POSHAN Abhiyaan as a commitment to improving nutrition and health outcomes in India, PM Modi recognized the need to make citizens responsible for the success of the initiative. The initiative was intended to be more than just a government effort—it aimed to become a people's movement that involved raising awareness, volunteering and contributing to the cause. Mindful of the importance of nutrition for the overall development of India, PM Modi's *Mann Ki Baat* stepped in to fill the gap between government intervention and social change.

While we are on the subject of health, I would like to talk about one more issue. I feel very concerned about the lives of pregnant women of our country. In our country, close to 3 crore women become pregnant every year but some of these mothers die during childbirth. Sometimes the mother loses her life, at times the infant does. There are times when both die. It is true that in the last decade there has been a decline in maternal mortality rates but even now, we are not able to save the lives of a large number of pregnant women. Anaemia during or after pregnancy, pregnancy related infections, high BP, any such complication can have devastating effect. Keeping in view these issues, in the last few months, the Government of India has launched a new campaign 'Prime Minister Safe Motherhood Campaign'. Under this, on the 9th of every month, all pregnant women will get a check-up at government health centers free of cost. I urge all poor families to ensure that all pregnant women avail of this benefit on the 9th of every month, so that if by the time they reach the 9th month any complication arises, it can be dealt with suitably in time and the lives of both mother and child can be saved. I have specially asked the gynaecologists whether they could offer their services free on the 9th of every month, for the sake of under privileged mothers! Can't my doctor brothers and sisters spare just 12 days in a year for this service to the under privileged? Over the last few days, many have written to me. There are thousands of doctors who have implemented what I said. But India is such a vast country. We need lakhs of doctors to join this campaign. I do believe that you will indeed do so.[1]

---

[1] "PM's "Mann ki Baat" Programme on All India Radio', *PMIndia*, 31 July 2016, https://tinyurl.com/mtmks4vp. Accessed on 12 April 2023.

While speaking about the importance of women in the fight against Covid-19, *Mann Ki Baat* also cast a rare spotlight on the efforts of women health workers, doctors, nurses and others who were on the frontline of the battle against the virus. The PM highlighted the role of women in providing essential services and taking care of the elderly and children during the lockdown. He also praised the hard work of women in the agricultural sector in India, who play a major role in ensuring food security in the country, and referred to them as the backbone of the sector. He also mentioned that the government is organizing several initiatives to empower women in the agricultural sector.

One beneficiary of these initiatives is Tongbram Bijayashanti, an agriculture entrepreneur from Manipur, who says:

> Hailing from a remote rural area in Bishnupur District of Manipur, I took up the innovative initiative of making fabrics from the stem of lotus plants after a lot of research. This has led to creating job avenues for the local people of my area giving a new vista of earning income and improving their economic status. The special mention by the prime minister in his *Mann Ki Baat* on 27 September 2020 has tremendously increased the popularity of my products. I hope *Mann Ki Baat* continues to encourage and promote entrepreneurs like me in a similar manner in the days to come.[2]

Prime Minister Modi recognizes the crucial role played by Bijayashanti and other such working-class women. To support them, he took to *Mann Ki Baat* to create awareness of the decision

---

[2]As told to Doordarshan in March 2023.

to give maternity leave of 26 weeks instead of 12 weeks as per earlier policies:

> There are now only two or three countries in the world that are ahead of us in this matter. India has taken a very important decision for these working women sisters of ours. The basic aim is to ensure proper care of the newborn, the future citizen of India, from the time of birth. The newborn should get the complete love and attention of the mother. That is how these children will become true assets of the country when they grow up. Mothers too will remain healthy. And that is why, this is such a landmark decision, and this will benefit 18 lakh women working in the formal sector.[3]

SALUTE TO *STREE SHAKTI*

Independent India has had a long history of women's empowerment. Prime Minister Modi brought to light its little-known aspects, including India's participation in the UN shaped by iconic women leaders:

> A unique feature related to the United Nations is that the woman power of India has played a large role in increasing the influence and strength of the United Nations.
>
> In 1947–48, when the Universal Declaration of UN Human Rights was being drafted, it was being inscribed in that Declaration "All Men are Created Equal". But a Delegate from

---

[3]"PM's "Mann ki Baat" Programme on All India Radio', *PMIndia*, 26 March 2017, https://tinyurl.com/mr2vxhr8. Accessed on 12 April 2023.

India objected to this and then it was written in the Universal Declaration—"All Human Beings are Created Equal". This was in consonance with India's age-old tradition of gender equality. Did you know that Smt. Hansa Mehta was the delegate because of whom this became possible? At the same time, another delegate Smt. Lakshmi Menon had strongly put forth her views on the issue of gender equality. And not only this, in 1953, Smt. Vijaya Lakshmi Pandit became the first woman President of the UN General Assembly.[4]

Marking International Women's Day has been a consistent annual theme of *Mann Ki Baat* over the past nine years with the ninety-ninth episode in March 2023 dedicating substantial time to women achievers across India. Over these nine years, the PM has spoken of the need to celebrate the courage, determination and hard work of women, noting that their contributions to society should be acknowledged. Across multiple episodes, he highlighted the success of women in various fields, such as sports, science and technology, and expressed his appreciation for the efforts of women in the armed forces. In one such episode, Flying Officers Bhawana Kanth, Avani Chaturvedi and Mohana Singh came in for special praise on *Mann Ki Baat* as they breached glass ceilings and overcame gender barriers to take to the high skies in the latest fighter jets of the Indian Air Force.

The PM also spoke about the Indian naval sailing vessel (INSV) *Tarini*, the first female-crewed naval vessel to circumnavigate the globe as part of India's Navika Sagar Parikrama. The PM complimented the crew of the vessel, who made the nation

---

[4]"PM's Address in the 82nd Episode of "Mann Ki Baat'", *PMIndia*, 24 October 2021, https://tinyurl.com/bdzrrnjv. Accessed on 12 April 2023.

proud and wrote a new chapter in the history of the Indian Navy. He highlighted their achievements, noting that they had circumnavigated the globe in a record time of nine months and had even made it to the southernmost tip of the world, Antarctica. He also noted that the crew had visited several foreign ports and had been welcomed warmly everywhere they went. Additionally, he highlighted the pioneering spirit, courage, determination and hard work of the crew of INSV *Tarini*, noting that they had not only overcome numerous difficulties during the voyage but also performed various tasks, such as ship maintenance, navigation and navigation-related operations, under extremely challenging circumstances. He further noted that the crew had been able to perform all these tasks with remarkable efficiency and skill and had completed their mission successfully.

Consistently drawing on the experiences of women achievers, *Mann Ki Baat* has sought to inspire girls across India by holding up these achievers as role models with PM Modi's ministerial colleagues, such as Nirmala Sitharaman and (late) Sushma Swaraj, finding praise on the radio programme. Putting the spotlight on young girl achievers, in February 2020, 12-year-old Kamya Karthikeyan, a student of Navy Children's School, Mumbai, who set a record as the youngest mountaineer to scale the 6,962 m high Mount Aconcagua in South America, was the subject of praise for both her grit and fitness:

> Kamya's achievement also motivates everyone to stay fit. Fitness has also contributed in great measure in Kamya's achieving great heights at such a young age. A Nation that is fit, will always be a nation that is a hit.[5]

---

[5]"PM's Address in the 9th Episode of "Mann Ki Baat 2.0"", *PMIndia*, 23 February

Mountaineer Poorna Malavath from Telangana, who completed the Seven Summits Challenge and had the rare distinction of scaling Mount Everest at the young age of 13, also came in for praise on *Mann Ki Baat* in June 2022 after having scaled Mount Denali, the highest peak in North America.

SECOND ENGINE FOR DRIVING INCLUSION

If harnessing *stree shakti* (women's power) for nation-building was one engine of PM Modi's inclusive thrust for *Mann Ki Baat*, his consistent championing of disabled people as equal participants in the developmental journey of India was the second engine for driving inclusion.

> Another thing came to my mind for the specially-abled. And among them especially from the kin of visually impaired, they made quite a number of phone calls. The reason may be that they are not able to watch TV, but they must definitely be listening to the radio. This made me realize how important the radio is for the visually impaired people. I am seeing a new aspect and they put forth such good suggestions that they are enough to make the governments more sensitive.[6]

Prime Minister Modi has consistently addressed the concerns of disabled people. He has emphasized the need to create a more inclusive and accessible society that recognizes their potential and

2020, https://tinyurl.com/4au94waw. Accessed on 12 April 2023.

[6]"English Rendering of Text of Prime Minister's "Mann Ki Baat" on All India Radio on 20th September 2015', *PMIndia*, 20 September 2015. https://tinyurl.com/yc37ktn6. Accessed on 12 April 2023.

limitations. Intrinsic to this effort has been his coinage of the term 'divyang', in an attempt to shift the focus from disability to the unique abilities and strengths of these individuals. It is derived from the Sanskrit words *divya*, which means divine, and *anga*, which means body part. In this context, it suggests that those with disabilities have a divine aspect to their abilities. It can be seen as a more positive and empowering term that highlights the strengths and unique capabilities of individuals. While there is a debate on this term and its shortcomings, it has, however, helped challenge stereotypes to change the way society views and interacts with people with disabilities.

One of the key initiatives that PM Modi has discussed is the Accessible India Campaign, which aims to make government buildings, transportation and information and communication technology more accessible for disabled individuals.

In addition to these initiatives, the PM has also used *Mann Ki Baat* to highlight the achievements and stories of disabled people who have overcome the challenges of being in an able-bodied world and made significant contributions to society. He has shared stories of individuals who have excelled in sports, arts and other fields and emphasized the importance of celebrating and supporting their achievements.

As a champion for para-sports and para-sportspersons, every medal and event has been a cause for celebration on *Mann Ki Baat*. Discussing India's achievements at the 2018 Asian Para Games, where Indian para-athletes won a total of 72 medals, PM Modi congratulated all participants for their hard work and dedication. He also mentioned that the Asian Para Games had increased India's profile in the para-sports world and raised the bar for future athletes. The PM praised the courage, determination and achievements of Deepa Malik, who won a silver medal at the 2016 Summer Paralympics in Rio de Janeiro, and noted that her success was an inspiration to all Indians. He also remarked that she had become a role model for people all over the world. Speaking about the commitment to create a supportive and enabling environment for disabled athletes so that they can achieve their full potential, PM Modi's personal championing of para-sports and para-sportspersons, such as Devendra Jhajharia, Mariyappan Thangavelu, Varun Singh Bhati and Jigar Thakker, is without a parallel during the seven decades of independent India. This celebration of para-athletes has motivated and inspired many people with disabilities to take up para-sports, as shared by Paralympics medallist Sumit Antil, in a conversation with an online sports news portal.[7]

Paying tribute to the can-do attitude of disabled people, *Mann Ki Baat* recalled how a team of disabled youth scaled the Siachen glacier. Recounting the grit and determination of these courageous individuals—Mahesh Nehra and Akshat Rawat from Uttarakhand, Pushpak Gawande from Maharashtra, Ajay Kumar from Haryana, Lobsang Chospel from Ladakh, Major Dwarkesh from Tamil Nadu, Irfan Ahmed Mir from Jammu and Kashmir and Chongjin Ingmo from Himachal Pradesh—PM Modi stated that the operation to scale the Siachen glacier was made successful because of the veterans of the special forces of the Indian Army who helped this group in its endeavour.[8]

Beyond para-sports, Javed Ahmed, a terror victim who lost his limbs, found mention on *Mann Ki Baat* for running a school for

[7]Jha, Tarkesh, 'Meeting PM Modi Was a Big Moment, Notes Paralympics Medalist Sumit Antil', *Khel Now*, 26 December 2022, https://tinyurl.com/bdhjpuhz. Accessed on 12 April 2023.

[8]'PM Modi Lauds Team of Differently-Abled People for Hoisting Flag at Siachen', *ANI*, 26 September 2021, https://tinyurl.com/ts4z3wdn. Accessed on 14 April 2023.

the disabled at Bijbehara in Jammu and Kashmir. Dilip Chauhan, a visually challenged school teacher in Ahmedabad, saw global recognition for his efforts to celebrate World Disability Day at his school, making accessibility his mission by gathering a few thousand children and making them aware about accessibility for disabled people. The media coverage of speech-challenged eight-year-old Tushar's efforts at putting a stop to his community's practice of open defecation by using a whistle is a testament to how inclusion on *Mann Ki Baat* is not merely about people with disabilities overcoming their limitations but also about demonstrating that they are an integral part of community initiatives and can play the role of agents of change:

> It was a very emotional moment for me. Government of India had organized a Mega Camp for Divyang persons and a number of world records were established that day. A visually challenged little girl child Gauri Shardul, hailing from far flung forest area in the Dang District, can recite the complete Ramayana epic as she has learnt it by heart. She rendered certain portions before me and when I presented her performance before other persons there, everyone was amazed.[9]

WHEN INCLUSION BECOMES INTRINSIC

Community initiatives towards inclusion of disabled people have seen significant momentum with *Mann Ki Baat* giving

---

[9]"PM's "Mann ki Baat" Programme on All India Radio on 25 September, 2016', *PMIndia*, 25 September 2016, https://tinyurl.com/4fdubpff. Accessed on 12 April 2023.

them space and spotlight. In fact, the programme has emerged as a comprehensive encyclopaedia of sorts, documenting community-led change efforts across India, from remote tribal hamlets to residential associations in mega cities. Considering the efforts of the Indian Sign Language Research and Training Center and the organization of an art gallery by the Voice of SAP to display works created by people with disabilities, community efforts at inclusion have shown the way for how this mass movement towards positive change can be sustained despite several limiting challenges. Yet another example is the effort to make the oldest Assamese dictionary, Hemkosh, visually accessible in braille spanning more than 10,000 pages in 15 volumes. One more such community-led initiative aimed at providing education to street children and slum dwellers in New Delhi was the focus of *Mann Ki Baat* in April 2018. Starting with just 15 children from the slums near Geeta Colony in New Delhi, the initiative is being run at 12 additional places and has touched the lives of more than 2,000 underprivileged children, with young teachers taking two hours from their busy schedules to bringing about a social transformation.

Taking the message of inclusion within communities beyond charitable activities, *Mann Ki Baat* has also spoken about fundamental changes in attitudes, where the spirit of inclusion is deepened within communities and families are sensitized to be inclusive in different aspects of everyday life. Reflecting this was PM Modi's call to action in October 2020, ahead of the first festival season during the Covid-19 pandemic, which saw extended periods of lockdown. With the pandemic impacting local businesses and service providers, PM Modi called upon communities to be vocal about shopping local to support the local businesses, while also urging families to spare a thought for the local service providers who continued to provide essential services during the lockdown. From sanitation workers and domestic help to local vegetable vendors, milkmen and security guards, PM Modi encouraged making all who provided essential services without a break a part of the festivities. In his plea to the communities to consider them as members of the family, inclusion became a mantra for healing the fabric of society that was frayed by the pandemic's devastating effects.

Over the years, *Mann Ki Baat* has emerged as a platform for janbhagidari or community participation. When the PM spoke about Indian toys, the communities that were directly involved in toy making not only saw an immediate socio-economic impact, but also found themselves embracing digital commerce and reducing India's dependency on imports and thereby becoming agents of change. *Mann Ki Baat*'s championing of Indian genres of storytelling brought families and communities together to rediscover folk wisdom and the treasure trove of content in native languages. There have been many such moments over the almost-hundred-episode saga of the programme, in which public participation and collective effort have played a significant role. Notable among such community-led efforts to feature on *Mann Ki Baat* was Mission Jal Thal in Kashmir:

This is a unique effort to clean the lakes and ponds of Srinagar and restore their old glory. The focus of 'Mission Jal Thal' is on 'Kushal Saar' and 'Gil Saar'. Along with public participation, a lot of help of technology is also being taken in this. To find out where there has been encroachment, where illegal construction has taken place, a formal survey of this area was carried out. Along with this, a campaign to remove plastic waste and clean up the waste was also launched. In the second phase of the mission, a lot of effort was also made to restore the old water channels and 19 springs filling the lake. In order to spread more and more awareness about the importance of this Restoration Project, local people and youth were also made water ambassadors. Now the local people here are also taking efforts for increasing the number of migratory birds and fish in 'Gil Saar Lake' and are also happy to see it.[10]

Aijaz Asad, the district magistrate of Srinagar, has experienced the impact of *Mann Ki Baat* in furthering inclusivity in the valley first-hand. According to Asad, the community-led efforts to restore the Gil Sar and Khushal Sar lakes, nearly 30 years after these water bodies had become extinct, was a direct result of the call to action by PM Modi. It also inspired a Tiranga Shikara Rally by the citizens of Srinagar in the famous Dal Lake. As per Asad, the most notable effect was the immense boost to tourism in the valley thanks to the blooming Tulip Gardens, which received wide attention through *Mann Ki Baat* and directly impacted the local community with economic opportunities.[11]

The entire country has embraced conservation through inclusion and community-led action, as local communities from Kashmir in the north to the islands of Lakshadweep in the south have found a national platform to exchange experiences and best practices. Speaking of preservation of local arts and culture by youth of the islands, PM Modi highlighted a club called the Kummel Brothers Challengers Club being run in Kalpeni, Lakshwadeep. The club trains youth in local art forms

---

[10]'PM's Address in the 86th Episode of "Mann Ki Baat"', *PMIndia*, 27 February 2022, https://tinyurl.com/2bcdd47h. Accessed on 12 April 2023.
[11]In conversation with the author in March 2023.

of Kolkali, Parichakli and Kilipaat in an effort to preserve the heritage of the island's communities. When floods hit Gujarat during the monsoon season of 2017, *Mann Ki Baat* lauded the communities that came together to clean up after the flood-waters had receded. Dhanera in the Banaskantha district of Gujarat saw volunteers of Jamiat Ulama-i-Hind clean 22 affected temples as well as two mosques in a phased manner. Prime Minister Modi described this as an inspiring example of unity for cleanliness and conservation of heritage sites achieved through inclusive community-led efforts.

Mann Ki Baat has been steadfast in nudging behavioural changes, shaping societal attitudes and breaking taboos. While much of the mainstream attention has been on the macro issues and community action on the big campaigns, it is noteworthy how PM Modi never lost sight of the small issues—the little things that matter to those at the margins of society. It is perhaps a reflection of his own life journey and the formative experiences from his early life that he not only ensured these little things received national attention through *Mann Ki Baat* but did so with a mantra of positivity rather than through emotions of victimhood. It was these very formative life experiences that manifested themselves in his call to action in August 2017, when he urged citizens to resist the temptation to haggle and bargain with small vendors, over a few rupees. Striking an emotive tone, he asked his listeners to think about what may be going through the minds of the small vendors when the well-to-do haggle. Expressing deep empathy for these small vendors who are at the receiving end of such behaviour, he spoke about the feeling of hurt over questioning the honesty of the vendor and the heartache caused by such pettiness within society. Readers will also recall an earlier instance when PM Modi called on families to be inclusive while celebrating festivals.

The profoundness of these remarks needs to be understood from the vantage point of a younger PM Modi growing up in a humble household, observing societal behaviour and absorbing its vicissitudes; while his mother worked as a domestic help to make ends meet and his father vended tea at the railway station to make a living. It is to the credit of values inculcated during his formative years that empathy and positivity took root within him, to inspire and lead a mass movement for societal change many decades later from politics to parliament.

With his inclusive legislative agenda reflecting social priorities, PM Modi's *Mann Ki Baat* has been a continuous commentary on transcending partisan politics in the interest of the greater good.

This Monsoon session of Parliament will always be remembered as a session for social justice and youth welfare. A number of important bills beneficial to the youth and the backward classes were passed during this session. As you know, a demand to constitute an OBC Commission similar to SC/ST commission was long pending for decades. The country fulfilled its resolve this time to make an OBC Commission and also granted it Constitutional powers. This step will prove to be the one to move forward our march towards achieving the goal of social justice. An amendment bill to secure the rights of scheduled castes and scheduled tribes also were passed in this session. This Act will give more security to the interests of SC and ST communities. This will also forbid criminals from indulging in atrocities and will instill confidence among the dalit communities.

No civil society can tolerate any kind of injustice towards the woman-power of the country. The nation will not tolerate those committing rapes. With this point in view Parliament has made a provision of strictest punishment by passing the Criminal Act Amendment Bill. Those guilty of rape will get a minimum sentence of ten years and those found guilty of raping girls below the age of 12 years will be awarded the death sentence. Recently, you might have read in newspapers, that a court in Mandsaur in Madhya Pradesh, after a brief hearing of two months, pronounced the death sentence on two criminals found guilty of raping a minor girl. Earlier, a court in Katni in Madhya Pradesh awarded the death sentence to the guilty after a hearing of just five days. Courts in Rajasthan have also taken similar quick decisions. This Act will play an effective role in curbing crimes against women and girls. Economic growth will be incomplete without a social transformation. The Triple Talaq Bill has been passed by the Lok Sabha although it could not be passed in the Rajya Sabha, I assure the Muslim women that the whole country stands by them to provide them social justice. When we move ahead in the national interest, a change in the lives of the poor, the backward, the exploited and the deprived ones can also be brought about.[12]

---

[12]'PM's "Mann ki Baat" Programme on All India Radio', *PMIndia*, 26 August 2018, https://tinyurl.com/z6v387kw. Accessed on 12 April 2023.

CHAPTER 13

DEMOCRACY GOES DIGITAL

I t would not be an exaggeration to characterize PM Modi as India's first digital PM. His penchant for digital technologies precedes his tenures in public office both as PM and CM. A rare late 1990s TV interview by then anchor and now Congress politician Rajeev Shukla with then BJP general secretary Narendra Modi reveals how he took to the Internet very early in his political career.[1] His tenure as the CM of Gujarat saw many digital firsts—from the use of Twitter to communicate directly with his constituents to the use of YouTube for live streaming of public events. A Google+ Hangout with him in 2012 saw Google's servers in India crash, unable to handle the traffic load.

Prime Minister Modi's embrace of digital technologies, both during electioneering and in government, saw the advent of a volunteer digital platform, MyGov, which has since become the bulwark of *Mann Ki Baat*. It marked the advent of an active

---

[1] 'Narendra Modi Was Like All of Us When It Comes to the Internet, Watch Old Clip Where He Revealed It Kept Him Awake Late at Nights', *OpIndia*, 13 November 2021, https://tinyurl.com/yt7x2zzd. Accessed on 19 April 2023.

participatory role for citizens of a digital India in governance using the Internet anytime, anywhere. The PM has since presided over the digitalization of the world's largest democracy. *Mann Ki Baat* has played twin roles of an illustrative example of participatory governance in a digital India and a catalyst for India's march towards becoming a digital democracy.

> In a democracy the power of the people is of great significance. This thought has been fundamental to my thinking and that is why I have immense faith in the power of the people. But with Mann Ki Baat whatever I was taught, whatever I was explained and the experiences I had, made me realize that the power of the people is limitless and it far exceeds our thinking. Our ancestors would say that there is a divine element in each individual. My experience of 'Mann Ki Baat' made me realize that the thinking of our ancestors was very powerful and had great authenticity in them as I have myself experienced them. I asked for suggestions for 'Mann Ki Baat' and yet could touch upon just 3–4 of them. But people continued to contribute actively in lakhs. This in itself is a great power. I did not feel that anyone got disheartened thinking that I wrote a letter to the PM or posted on mygov.in, yet my suggestions were not accepted even once.[2]

Prime Minister Modi's vision for a digital India has been about leveraging the Internet and digital technologies to connect people and improve access to information and services. For

---

[2]"English Rendering of Text of Prime Minister's "Mann Ki Baat" on All India Radio on 20th September 2015', *PMIndia*, 20 September 2015. https://tinyurl.com/yc37ktn6. Accessed on 12 April 2023.

him, a digital India is a step towards ensuring that everyone in India has access to the world of knowledge and opportunity, thus emerging as a major driver of economic growth. Continually urging the citizens to learn about the Internet and use it to access information, including government services, *Mann Ki Baat* has led by example.

Focussing on digital literacy and bridging the digital divide, the programme has been instrumental in putting the spotlight on how citizens from different walks of life not only learned how to use digital technologies and services but also contributed to the growth of digital India. The example that stands out is *Mann Ki Baat*'s championing of a cashless society and digital payments. It is instructive how PM Modi leveraged Dr B.R. Ambedkar as a symbol of equality and fraternity to project the Bharat Interface for Money (BHIM) app as a key enabler of a cashless society. The Unified Payment Interface (UPI) system, which allows people to transfer money easily and directly, has recorded monthly transactions in crores, with service charges for digital payments through BHIM and UPI waived off. Going beyond the BHIM app and payments, *Mann Ki Baat* also drew attention to the digitization of toll payments using FASTag as well as digitization of procurement across the government using the Government e Marketplace (GeM) portal.

The PM has drawn both national and global attention to India's digital public goods infrastructure with the trinity of direct benefits transfer, Aadhaar and UPI emerging as a game changer for India throughout the pandemic. Making the case for a digital India to check black money and tax evasion, *Mann Ki Baat* was instrumental in amplifying the long-term benefits of digital payments in reducing inflation, better targeting subsidies and making the economy more efficient. The consistent focus on the shift towards a digital cashless society can be seen across episodes of *Mann Ki Baat,* spanning more than a year, and drawing the attention of listeners to promotional schemes and incentives for making payments through the UPI.

The digitalization of the Indian democracy is best understood from the experiences of Isak Munda, Setha Singh Rawat and Omprakash Singh. Odia YouTuber Isak Munda, who was making a living as a daily wage labourer, caught the attention of the nation, when PM Modi highlighted his YouTube channel and how the creator economy on the Internet had empowered him. A year later, Munda's YouTube channel had more than 8 lakh subscribers with his most popular videos having registered more than 10 crore views. Similarly, Setha Singh Rawat, a tailor from Ajmer city in Rajasthan, saw his online portal Darji Online featured on *Mann Ki Baat*, highlighting how e-commerce had come to the aid of India's small businesses and self-employed service providers. Om Prakash Singh, a digital entrepreneur from Unnao in Uttar Pradesh, became a job creator by providing broadband Internet connections and Wi-Fi services in rural areas.

However, it is the story of a 'cashless day out' narrated by PM Modi that is most striking:

> Friends, can you imagine that someone could come out of one's house with a resolve that one would roam the whole city for the whole day without doing any money transaction in cash—isn't this an interesting resolve. Two daughters of Delhi, Sagarika and Preksha, experimented with Cashless Day Out like this. Wherever Sagarika and Preksha went in Delhi, they got the facility of digital payment. Because of the UPI QR code, they did not have to withdraw cash.

Even at most of the street food and roadside vendors they got the facility of online transaction.[3]

Mann Ki Baat's digital outreach crossed borders to engage the diaspora. Turning brain drain into brain gain was the voluntary digital effort of two Indian–American IT professionals with roots in Uttar Pradesh. Hailing from Raebareli, Rajnish Bajpai and Yogesh Sahu made a unique attempt to develop an app to bring digital technology to village democracy. Their joint efforts resulted in the development of the SmartGaon app, which not only utilized their professional skills but also tapped into their passion for rural development. Residents of the village Taudhakpur in Raebareli, the village chief, the district magistrate, the chief development officer and many others joined in to create awareness among the masses. The app demonstrated how a digital revolution was in the making in the village. With the help of this app, it became easier to record, track and monitor developmental work being done in the village. The app was very useful to the farmers as it enabled a digital marketplace of sorts, for produce.

If you look into this incident minutely, one thing will strike you and that is the young man living in America adhering to that country's lifestyle and ideology, who left India many years ago but, knows the finer details about his village, knows about the challenges and still is emotionally attached to his village. This seems to be the reason as to how he could develop this App which is most suited to needs of the village.[4]

[3]"PM's Address in the 88th Episode of "Mann Ki Baat"', *PMIndia*, 24 April 2022, https://tinyurl.com/4ad3w43t. Accessed on 12 April 2023.
[4]"PM's Mann Ki Baat Programme on All India Radio', *PMIndia*, 29 July 2018, https://tinyurl.com/2p8apx8f. Accessed on 12 April 2023.

Mann Ki Baat also became a platform for digital education, cautioning senior citizens and others against the perils of new age cybercrimes and financial fraud online, with PM Modi raising awareness on precautions to be taken.

> These are new methods of technology that are spreading in the entire world for cheating people. And just as technology plays an increasingly bigger role in our economic system, it also invites those who misuse it. A retired gentleman, who not only had to get his daughter married but also to build his home, one day he received an SMS, that there was a gift that had arrived from abroad and could be obtained if he deposited 2 lakh rupees as custom duty in a bank account and this gentlemen without giving any thought took out 2 lakh rupees from his hard-earned life savings and sent it to some stranger. That too on the strength of just an SMS! And in very little time, he understood that he had been looted! You too must be getting similarly confused sometimes! These people write a letter in such style that it seems perfect. They use fake letter pads while sending these letters. They obtain your credit card number and debit card number and empty your bank account through technology. And this new means of fraud is digital fraud. I believe that we must be aware against such lure, must remain cautious and if such false communications come to our notice, then we must share them with our friends and make them aware also.[5]

---

[5]PM's "Mann ki Baat" Programme on All India Radio', *PMIndia*, 31 July 2016, https://tinyurl.com/mtmks4vp. Accessed on 12 April 2023.

MORE THAN JUST APPS AND TRANSACTIONS

Digitalization of the Indian democracy during the nine years of PM Modi's premiership has not meant only apps and transactions, but more importantly, direct digital engagement of citizens in the process of lawmaking.

> Our pledge was to promote citizen participation in democracy and connect every citizen in the development work. And today I am pleased to share this after one year that nearly two crore people have visited MyGov website. We have received comments from five and a half lac people and I am extremely glad to mention that more than fifty thousand people took out time from their precious schedule to apply their mind and provide their suggestions on PMO applications as they considered this work important. And we have received quite significant suggestions.... We are receiving quite positive suggestions on MyGov, it is helping in getting assistance in creating logos, tag-lines and formulating policies by yourselves. We are experiencing fresh air in the administrative system. We are experiencing a new sense of consciousness.[6]

Mann Ki Baat was also witness to the entire life cycle of lawmaking, taking every section of the society along through the legislative process to educate, inform and raise awareness through the radio programme. The land acquisition ordinance and the farm laws were two occasions when PM Modi deferred to public opinion to alter

---

[6]"English Rendering of Prime Minister's "Mann ki Baat" on All India Radio', *PMIndia*, 26 July 2015, https://tinyurl.com/2w9wc9md. Accessed on 12 April 2023.

the course of legislature. On both occasions, *Mann Ki Baat* was a witness to the process, a medium to engage with the process and a listening post to close the feedback loop. On both occasions, the case for reforms was made to persuade the citizens.

The *Mann Ki Baat* episode of March 2015 was quite extraordinary for multiple reasons. It was a rare instance when a single topic consumed the entirety of an episode. It was also unique for the forthright manner in which myth after myth was dispelled to make the case for legislation that was pending in Parliament directly to the people. The episode also set a new democratic benchmark for how to make the case for a complex legislative reform to the citizens by explaining it in simple terms and taking on critics to counter their arguments with facts and logic.

In the case of the land acquisition ordinance, PM Modi's assurances of justice done and mistakes rectified to the farmers of India spoke of how the radio programme had become integral to the consultation mechanism for complex legislations that impacted the livelihood of crores across India.

Irrespective of the ultimate legislative fate of these measures, it was on *Mann Ki Baat* that the most forceful arguments in their support were recorded for posterity by PM Modi, in his own words, making it clear that in a democracy, the buck stops with the PM. Not shying away from constructive criticism, PM Modi also took to *Mann Ki Baat* to seek an honest appraisal of his government's decisions.

My dear countrymen, an audit and assessment of the performance of the present government in the last three years is happening all over on newspapers, social media or TV for the last 15 days. Three years ago, you vested the responsibility of 'Pradhan Sewak'—the Chief Servant of the

People upon me. There have been many surveys and several opinion polls. I see this entire process as a very healthy sign. The works done during these years were tested on every touch stone. It was analyzed by every segment of society. And this is a great process in democracy. I firmly believe that governments must be accountable in democracy and the public at large must be provided with report card of works done. I wish to congratulate those who took out time for an in-depth analysis of our work, there were some praises some support and sometimes shortcomings were also pointed out, I understand the importance of all these things. I thank those people, who provided critical and important feedback. The mistakes and the shortcomings once highlighted can be rectified. Whether something is good, little less effective or bad, whatever it is, one has to learn from it and move ahead in life putting the learning from it into practice.

Constructive criticism strengthens democracy; for an aware nation, an awakened nation, this churning is very important.[7]

The discourse on contemporary reform in the functioning of Indian democracy was not limited to PM Modi's government. He also spoke at length on crucial decisions taken during the Vajpayee era in Parliament starting with the Constitution (Ninety-First Amendment) Act, 2003. Highlighting its impact, he spoke about how reforms of the Vajpayee government have ensured a smaller cabinet size and a higher bar for defections across parties in legislatures.

---

[7]'PM's "Mann ki Baat" Programme on All India Radio', *PMIndia*, 28 May 2017, https://tinyurl.com/4sc3ex6m. Accessed on 12 April 2023.

For many years in India, the political culture of forming a very large cabinet was being misused to constitute jumbo cabinets not only to create a divide but also to appease political leaders. Atalji changed it. This effort of his resulted in saving of money as well as of resources. This also helped in improving efficiency. It could only be a visionary like Atalji who brought in this transformation and as a result of this, healthy traditions blossomed in our polity.[8]

KNOW YOUR CONSTITUTION

Strengthening local democracy with digital technologies, in many ways, helped realize the dreams of the constitution-makers of India. Viewing the Constitution as the foundation of our democracy and as the source of rights and freedoms, *Mann Ki Baat* sensitized listeners to how the unity and integrity of India was ensured by the Constitution. Citing it as the source of national strength and progress, the PM said that the Constitution inspired a national identity and motivated national pride. His discourse on the Constitution also informed and educated listeners on the makers of the Constitution, foremost among them being its chief architect, Dr B.R. Ambedkar, and his closely held constitutional values:

This is the day to remember the members of the Constituent Assembly. They all worked hard for about three years to draft the Constitution. And, whoever reads that debate will feel proud about what actually the vision of a life dedicated to

[8]PM's "Mann ki Baat" Programme on All India Radio', *PMIndia*, 26 August 2018, https://tinyurl.com/z6v387kw. Accessed on 12 April 2023.

the nation is. Can you imagine how hard their task would have been to frame the Constitution of our country which has such big diversities? They must have shown a great sense of understanding and farsightedness and that too at a juncture when the country was getting rid of the bondage of slavery. Now, this is the responsibility of all of us to make a New India in the light of the thinking of the makers of our Constitution. Our Constitution is all encompassing. There probably is no area, no aspect of nature which remained untouched.[9]

Mann Ki Baat has also contributed to the significant shift in the public discourse regarding the Indian Constitution in recent years, with fundamental duties getting their due alongside fundamental rights. Calling upon the citizens for ideas on fundamental duties, PM Modi, in the December 2015 episode of *Mann Ki Baat*, underlined how little of the public discourse focussed on them as compared to fundamental rights. His call to action on fundamental duties sought to raise public awareness on the Indian Constitution as the nation was set to mark the 125th birth anniversary of the constitution's chief architect, Dr B.R. Ambedkar. Over the nine years of *Mann Ki Baat*, fundamental duties have been a recurrent theme, consistent with PM Modi's untiring efforts to instil a sense of civic responsibility in a wide range of areas from cleanliness to respect for animals.

Over the years, *Mann Ki Baat* has been as much a celebration of democracy as it has been a cautionary periodic reminder of the darkest period of Indian democracy when fundamental rights

---

[9]'English Rendering of PM's Mann Ki Baat Programme on All India Radio', *PMIndia*, 26 November 2017, https://tinyurl.com/5ykyzy99. Accessed on 12 April 2023.

had been suspended through the exercise of Emergency powers. Media freedom was curtailed and political opposition was jailed. Reminding his listeners of the pivotal role played by the former PM Morarji Desai, PM Modi recalled the fight against Emergency and for the restoration of democracy.

> To save democracy, Morarji Desai flung himself in the movement against imposition of Emergency. For this, he had to pay a heavy price in his old age. The government of that time arrested and incarcerated him. But when the Janata Party won the general elections in 1977, he became the Prime Minister of the country. During his tenure, the 44th constitutional amendment was introduced. This was important because the 42nd amendment which was brought during the emergency, curtailed the powers of the Supreme Court and implemented provisions which stood to violate our democratic values, was struck down. The 44th amendment, made it mandatory that the proceedings of Parliament and Legislative Assemblies were made public through the newspapers. This amendment, restored certain powers of Supreme Court and declared that the fundamental rights granted under Article 20 and 21 of the Constitution could not be abrogated during the Emergency.
>
> For the first time constitutional safeguards guaranteed that the President could only announce the emergency upon the written recommendation of the Cabinet, and that the period of emergency could not be extended more than six months at any stretch of time. In this way, Morarji Bhai ensured that the way democracy was assassinated in 1975 by imposition of emergency, could never be repeated again

in the future. The upcoming generations of our nation will always remember his priceless contribution in maintaining the sanctity of Indian democracy. Once again, I pay my homage to a great leader like him.[10]

The essence of democracy is the exercise of the fundamental right to franchise. *Mann Ki Baat* has been at the forefront of creating voter awareness. From celebrating National Voters' Day to extolling the role played by the Election Commission, the programme has been a vehicle to evoke curiosity regarding the electoral process in the young minds of first-time voters as well as a motivational guide to get them to register and vote. If today, India, as the planet's only billion-people democracy, has emerged as a beacon and a role model, a key contribution has been made by *Mann Ki Baat* acting as a nutritional supplement in boosting its health and energizing its vigour.

In a democracy, every voter determines the destiny of a country and this awareness is spreading gradually. The voting percentage is also increasing and for this I want to congratulate the Election Commission of India. Up until a few years back we saw that our election commission worked only as a regulator but it has changed a lot in the last few years. Today, our election commission does not work only as a regulator but has become a facilitator, has become voter-friendly and the voter is at the centre of all its policies and its ideologies. It is a great change but we need more than what election commission can do. We must mobilize schools, colleges and societies—we must spread awareness always,

[10]'PM's Mann Ki Baat Programme on All India Radio', *PMIndia*, 24 February 2019, https://tinyurl.com/37mcjwr3. Accessed on 12 April 2023.

not only during the time of elections. The voter's list must be updated, we must also keep a watch on it. This priceless right that I have, is it safe? Am I using it or not? We must all develop this habit. I hope that all the youngsters who have not been registered in the voter's list yet, get themselves registered and must vote too. I publicly say during elections that one must cast his vote before he eats his food. This is a holy act, everyone must do it.[11]

[11]'English Rendering of Text of Prime Minister's "Mann Ki Baat" on All India Radio on 20th September 2015', *PMIndia*, 20 September 2015. https://tinyurl.com/yc37ktn6. Accessed on 12 April 2023.

CHAPTER 14

A LIFELONG SEEKER OF KNOWLEDGE

India is a land of many languages, and each language has its own unique beauty and charm. The importance of language in preserving India's culture and heritage has been a continuing theme of PM Modi's public discourse over the years. The programme is perhaps the first and only public discourse of its kind that is available in more than 20 languages and several dialects. Researchers of AI use the multilingual text of the programme to develop and test machine translation capabilities.

MANY LANGUAGES, ONE EXPRESSION

Prime Minister Modi has always invoked India's rich linguistic diversity as a source of strength and a matter of celebration through *Mann Ki Baat*. This is as much about national unity in the spirit of EBSB as it is about boosting learning. Highlighting this diversity comprising hundreds of languages and thousands of dialects, spanning the geographic expanse of India—from Kashmir to Kanyakumari, from Kutch to Kohima—PM Modi reminded his listeners how they are mutually integrated: many languages, one expression.

His view of India's linguistic diversity was not of a static landscape frozen in time but that of a dynamic milieu constantly evolving whilst learning from each other, developing each other and refining themselves. He recalled that one of the world's oldest languages, Tamil, is as much of Indian origin, a source of pride and a significant component of India's heritage, as Sanskrit, which has given birth to many other Indian languages. With 121 categories of mother tongues and 13 scheduled languages, with more than 1 crore people in everyday life, *Mann Ki Baat*'s championing of India's languages has not just been a medium for expression, but also a means to preserve India's culture and heritage.

Prime Minister Modi ensured this by peppering *Mann Ki Baat* with memorable quotes across languages, texts and great works of literature. Drawing from Vedic literature in Sanskrit to Buddhist and Jain texts in Pali, *Mann Ki Baat*'s employment of quotes as a device to reach and connect with the masses is an encyclopaedic effort in itself. If the Ishopanishad inspired a quote to drive home the point regarding organ donations (October 2015 episode of *Mann Ki Baat*), the Bhagavad Gita reminded the importance of planting trees. Drawing extensively from Vedic literature and Sanskrit sources, PM Modi repeatedly put forward the innate Hindu ethic of living in harmony with nature to all of his listeners. Gender values and empowering the girl child saw a quote from the Skanda Purana to inspire listeners.[1] Additionally,

---

[1]'PM's Mann Ki Baat Programme on All India Radio', *PMIndia*, 28 January 2018, https://tinyurl.com/33b6v3c5. Accessed on 14 April 2023.

the Shanti Mantra from the Taittiriya Aranyaka made a universal appeal for world peace.[2]

The PM has also repeatedly quoted from celebrated poets, thinkers and icons from almost every region and every era of India. Amir Khusro's poetry on the change of seasons and Kabir's and Ravidas's dohas were timely reminders to listeners for issues like water conservation and overcoming caste divisions.[3] From Sanchi Honnamma's poem in Kannada to Avvaiyar's Tamil quote on biodiversity, *Mann Ki Baat* straddled India's linguistic diversity of writers, thinkers and poets.

Modern words of wisdom from Gurudev Rabindranath Tagore to inspirational verses of Atal Bihari Vajpayee—all made their appearance. Similarly, from Mahadevi Verma to Harivansh Rai Bachchan, modern poets and their works have also found an echo on the programme.

Prime Minister Modi's role in raising public consciousness of Sanskrit is a little-told story. From encouraging Sanskrit news presenters on Doordarshan to adopt a modern persona and consistently highlighting Sanskrit in *Mann Ki Baat*, he has emerged as one of Sanskrit's most passionate advocate. Sanskrit and Swahili earned their spotlight in January 2015 when PM Modi held a joint *Mann Ki Baat* with President Obama as he sought to draw parallels between the African notion of ubuntu and the ancient Indian notion of *vasudhaiva kutumbakam* (the entire planet is one family).

The Internet has, in many ways, lowered the barriers for learning and disseminating Sanskrit. Responding to a listener's

---

[2]'PM's Mann Ki Baat Programme on All India Radio', *PMIndia*, 28 October 2018, https://tinyurl.com/34wjw7ee. Accessed on 14 April 2023.
[3]'PM's "Mann Ki Baat" Programme on All India Radio', *PMIndia*, 24 June 2018, https://tinyurl.com/2d4b7ext. Accessed on 14 April 2023.

request for online Sanskrit courses, PM Modi, during *Mann Ki Baat* in March 2018, gave an open call to boost Internet-based Sanskrit learning. Such was the impact of the call to action that about nine months later, in December 2018, he was able to draw the attention of his listeners to the online web portal *Samskritabharati.in*. Sustaining the focus on Sanskrit, listeners and sports enthusiasts were treated to cricket commentary in Sanskrit in February 2021.

However, the highlight of *Mann Ki Baat's* focus on Sanskrit was the episode that aired in August 2018, in which PM Modi drew the attention of the listeners to Sanskrit Week celebrations, culminating in Sanskrit Day on Shravan Purnima (the full moon day of the Hindu calendar month of Shravan, which also marks the festival of Raksha Bandhan).

> I congratulate all those actively involved in preserving and conserving this glorious heritage, helping it to reach out to the masses. Every language has its own significance, sanctity. We Indians also feel proud that from Vedic times to the modern day, Sanskrit language has played a stellar role in the universal spread of knowledge.
>
> Sanskrit language and literature encompass a storehouse of knowledge pertaining to every facet of life. Science and technology, agriculture and health, mathematics and management, economy and environment, the entire spectrum has been touched upon. It is said that our Vedas have detailed reference on Mantras, on ways & means to counter the challenges of global warming. You will be pleased to know that even today, residents of village Mattur in Shivamogga district of Karnataka use Sanskrit as their lingua franca.

You will be astonished to know that Sanskrit is a language that possesses the capacity for infinite word formation with two thousand verb roots, 200 suffixes and 22 prefixes; coupled with compounds, the possibility of word-creation is limitless. And that is why the minutest nuance of an expression or subject can be accurately described. This has been the core speciality of Sanskrit. Today, at times, in order to communicate more assertively, we tend to make use of English Quotations or even sher-o-shayari-urdu poetry. But those who are well acquainted with Sanskrit Subhashitas—epigrammatic verses—know very well that it is possible to make a crisp, precise statement, using very few words through the usage of subhashitas. And since there is a sense of geographical and cultural belonging, they are easy to understand & assimilate.

For example, in order to illustrate the significance of the Guru in one's life, it has been said:

एकमपि अक्षरमस्तु गुरुः शिष्यं प्रबोधयेत् ।
प्रथिव्यां नास्ति तद्–दृव्यं, यद दृ दत्त्वा ह्यनृणीभवेत ।।

Thereby meaning, when a guru imparts even an iota of knowledge to the student, there is no material or wealth on the entire earth that the student can make use of, to repay the guru.[4]

In August 2021, *Mann Ki Baat* marked Sanskrit Day with an interesting experiment in community radio in Kevadia, home to the now world-famous Statue of Unity.

---

[4]"PM's "Mann ki Baat" Programme on All India Radio', *PMIndia*, 26 August 2018, https://tinyurl.com/epteac2p. Accessed on 13 April 2023.

नमोनमः सर्वेभ्यः। मम नाम गङ्गा। भवन्तः शृण्वन्तु रेडियो–युनिटी–नवति–
एफ.एम–'एकभारतं श्रेष्ठ–भारतम्'। अहम् एकतामूर्तेः मार्गदर्शिका
एवं रेडियो–
युनिटी–माध्यमे आर् जे. अस्मि। अद्य संस्कृतदिनम् अस्ति। सर्वेभ्यः बह्व्यः
शुभकामनाः सन्ति। सरदार–वल्लभभाई–पटेलमहोदयः 'लौहपुरुषः'
इत्युच्यते।। २०१३–
तमे वर्षे लौहसंग्रहस्य अभियानम् प्रारब्धम्। १३४–टन–परिमितस्य
लौहस्य गलनं
कृतम्। झारखण्डस्य एकः कृषकः मुद्गरस्य दानं कृतवान्। भवन्तः
शृण्वन्तु रेडियो–युनिटी–नवति–एफ.एम–'एकभारतं श्रेष्ठ–भारतम्'।

Friends, you must have understood the language. This was
Sanskrit being spoken on the radio and the one speaking
was RJ Ganga. RJ Ganga is a member of a group of Radio
Jockeys in Gujarat. Her other companions are RJ Neelam,
RJ Guru and RJ Hetal. All of them together in Gujarat, in
Kevadia are currently engaged in enhancing respect for the
Sanskrit language. And the radio jockeys are such that they
wear multiple hats simultaneously. They also serve as guides,
and also run the Community Radio Initiative, Radio Unity
90 FM. These RJs talk to their listeners in Sanskrit language,
providing them with information in Sanskrit.[5]

Further elaborating on the salience of Sanskrit, PM Modi had
this to share:

अमृतम् संस्कृतम् मित्र, सरसम् सरलम् वचः।
एकता मूलकम् राष्ट्रे, ज्ञान विज्ञान पोषकम्।

That is, our Sanskrit language is sweet and also simple.

---

[5]"PM's address in the 80th Episode of "Mann Ki Baat"", *PMIndia*, 29 August
2021, https://tinyurl.com/m42b2kb4. Accessed on 13 April 2023.

Sanskrit literature comprises the divine philosophy of humanity and knowledge which can captivate anyone's attention. Recently, I got to know about many such people who are engaged in the inspirational work of teaching Sanskrit in foreign lands. One such person is Mr. Rutger Kortenhorst, a well-known Sanskrit scholar and teacher in Ireland who teaches Sanskrit to the children there. Sanskrit language also plays an important role in the strengthening of cultural relations between India and Ireland and between India and Thailand here in the east. Dr. Chirapat Prapandavidya and Dr. Kusuma Rakshamani, both of them are playing a very important role in the promotion of Sanskrit language in Thailand. They have also carried out comparative studies in literature of Thai and Sanskrit languages. Another such professor is Shriman Boris Zakharin, who teaches Sanskrit at Moscow State University in Russia. He has published many research papers and books. He has also translated many books from Sanskrit to Russian. Likewise, Sydney Sanskrit School is one of Australia's premier institutions, where Sanskrit language is taught to the students. For children, these schools also organize programs like Sanskrit Grammar Camp, Sanskrit Plays and Sanskrit Day.

Friends, the efforts which have been made in recent times have brought a new awareness about Sanskrit. Now is the time to increase our efforts in this direction. It is our collective duty to cherish our heritage, preserve it, pass it on to the new generation.... and future generations also have a right to it. Now is the time to increase everyone's efforts for these works as well. Friends, if you know of any such person engaged in this kind of effort, if you have any such information, then please share the information related to them on social media with the hashtag Celebrating Sanskrit.[6]

From celebrating Sanskrit to expressing a special love for Tamil, *Mann Ki Baat*, in its ninety-sixth episode, drew attention to a unique amalgamation of India's civilizational symbols: the Kashi–Tamil Sangamam. Elaborating further on how Tamil language had transcended geographical constraints, the ninety-ninth episode of *Mann Ki Baat* in March of 2023 focussed on the Saurashtri Tamil community and the Saurashtra Tamil Sangam that was being held in different parts of the western Indian state of Gujarat.

Prime Minister Modi's championing of Tamil through *Mann Ki Baat* inspired Annamalai, who formerly served in the Indian Police Service, to undertake an initiative to popularize the language and its culture. In the true spirit of a karmayogi, Annamalai committed himself to champion unsung heroes of Tamil Nadu through his initiative, Ariyapadatha Athisaya Manithargal. Reflecting on the focus on Tamil culture in *Mann Ki Baat*, Annamalai recalled how a little-known dance form, Karakattam received national attention in February 2023. He also drew attention to the impact of *Mann Ki Baat*'s call to action on Thanjavur Thalaiyatti Bommais (Thanjavur dolls), resulting in increased purchase of the same. According to Annamalai, *Mann Ki Baat*'s exemplary focus on Tamil heroes, such as Veera Managai Rani Velu Nachiyar, foremost amongst women freedom fighters of India, has not only raised much needed national awareness but also brought to the fore PM Modi's deep appreciation and love for Tamil, thus dispelling many myths and misconceptions.[7]

---

[6]Ibid.
[7]In conversation with the author in March 2023.

Recognizing the power of language as the gateway to learning, *Mann Ki Baat*, over its journey of almost a hundred episodes, has drawn inspiration from these words of Subramania Bharati in Tamil to inspire, motivate and celebrate India's diverse linguistic heritage:

"The progress of one's language, is the source of one's overall progress

All progress is meaningless if one's mother tongue is neglected" [...]

முப்பது கோடி முகமுடை யாள். (Mupppadu kODi mugam uDai yaaL)

உயிர் மொய்ம்புற ஒன்றுடையாள் (uyir moim bura onDruDaiyaaL)

இவள் செப்பு மொழிபதி னெட்டுடையாள் (ivaL seppu mozhi padineTTuDaiyaaL)

எனில் சிந்தனை ஒன்றுடையாள் (enil sindanai onDruDaiyaaL) [...]

Mother India has 30 crore faces, but one body. She speaks 18 languages, but thinks as one.[8]

PRESERVING HERITAGE: ONE LANGUAGE AT A TIME

No literary effort was too small for *Mann Ki Baat*, with every attempt at preservation of scripts and dialects from every corner of India finding mention and being a subject of appreciation. The efforts of Sripati Tudu from Purulia (a district in West Bengal),

---

[8]"PM's Address in the 6th Episode of "Mann Ki Baat 2.0", *PMIndia*, 24 November 2019, https://tinyurl.com/4a5895vr. Accessed on 13 April 2023.

who was a professor at the Sidho-Kanho-Birsha University, caught PM Modi's attention in May 2022. Professor Tudu, who specializes in Santhali, a language spoken by several indigenous tribes of India, undertook the onerous task of translating and transcribing the Indian Constitution into the Ol Chiki script for the benefit of all Santhali citizens of India, from within various tribal communities.

With 2019 as the International Year of Indigenous Languages, *Mann Ki Baat's* call to action to conserve languages and dialects on the verge of extinction drew inspiration from the father of modern Hindi literature, Bhartendu Harishchandra, and also from Mahakavi Subramania Bharati.

Mann Ki Baat highlighted the cause of the Rang community's efforts to save its language. Dharchula in Uttarakhand, having Nepal on one side and Kali Ganga on the other, is home to the Rang community that converses amongst itself in the Ranglo language. With speakers of the language rapidly dwindling, the estimated 10,000-strong community undertook efforts with 84-year-old veterans like Diwan Singh to 22-year-olds like Vaishali contributing stories, poems and songs. Since the language did not have a script, social media became a kind of classroom, where everyone was a student and a teacher at the same time. Different kinds of programmes are being held and magazines are being published; social institutions are also assisting in this effort.

Taking the occasion of International Mother Language Day as an opportunity, PM Modi struck an emotive chord to make his case on the primacy of native tongue and the need to preserve India's rich heritage of languages and dialects.

Those who are learned can give a lot of academic input about where the word mother tongue came from, how it originated. I would emphasise about mother tongue that as our mother moulds our life, in the same manner, mother tongue also shapes our life. The mother and mother tongue, both together strengthen the foundation of life; lending it permanence. Just like we cannot abandon our mother, similarly, we cannot leave our mother tongue either.

I remember an incident of yesteryears, when I had gone to America, I would get a chance to visit different families. Once I went to a Telugu family and I got to see a very happy scenario there. They told me that they had made a rule in the family that no matter how busy one were to be, if they were not outstation, then all the family members would have dinner sitting at the table together and equally compulsory on the dinner table was conversing in Telugu language only. This was also the rule for the children who were born there. Seeing this love for the mother tongue, I was highly impressed by this family.[9]

LANGUAGE AND LEARNING

An emphasis on the importance of learning multiple languages stands out for its potential role in facilitating an understanding of different cultures and perspectives, thus promoting tolerance. At the intersection of boosting learning and preservation of

---

[9]"PM's Address in the 86th Episode of "Mann Ki Baat"", *PMIndia*, 27 February 2022, https://tinyurl.com/mrxr9zmf. Accessed on 13 April 2023.

linguistic heritage was PM Modi's endeavour to promote Indian languages as the medium of education through the National Education Policy (NEP). The NEP is being seen as a historic step towards transforming India's education system with the objective of bringing about a paradigm shift in the way education has traditionally been imparted in modern-day India. With the NEP's focus on holistic and multidisciplinary education and on the development of critical thinking, creativity and problem-solving skills in students, its thrust had twenty-first-century skills like communication, collaboration and digital literacy in its sights.

This shift in focus to native-language education is critical for many deprived families who, through sheer determination and perseverance, overcome all odds and aspire to learn.

> Examples such as Prince Kumar of Delhi, whose father is a DTC bus driver, Abhay Gupta of Kolkata who studied on foothpaths under street lights, Afreen Sheikh of Ahmedabad, whose father drives an auto rickshaw, Nagpur's daughter Khushi, whose father is a school bus driver, Karthik of Haryana, whose father is a watchman or Ramesh Sahu of Jharkhand, whose father is a brick-kiln labourer or Gurgaon's divyang angel Anushka Panda, who suffers from a hereditary disorder called spinal muscular atrophy... all of them overcame each & every obstacle through their firm resolve and Zeal, attaining success for the world to see. If we look around, we can see many such examples.[10]

---

[10]'PM's Mann Ki Baat Programme on All India Radio', *PMIndia*, 29 July 2018, https://tinyurl.com/2p9c3635. Accessed on 13 April 2023.

A lifetime of learning is not possible without valuing books and literature, as pointed out by PM Modi when he called for gifting books as an alternative to gifting bouquets:

> Recently, I had the opportunity to go to one of my favorite events. A very good programme is being run in Kerala for the past few years, by the P.N. Panicker Foundation, which encourages people to cultivate the habit of reading books and to enhance their awareness towards this, by organising celebrations such as 'Reading Day', and 'Reading Month'. I had the opportunity to go for the inaugural function, where I was told that instead of bouquets, they gift books. I liked it. Thus I was also reminded of what had slipped my mind. Because when I was in Gujarat, I had set this tradition of welcoming, by not giving bouquets, but books or handkerchiefs instead. And that too, a 'Khadi' handkerchief, so that it promotes 'Khadi'. Till the time I was in Gujarat, this habit had been ingrained in us, but after coming here, I had lost that habit. When I went to Kerala, it was rekindled. I have already begun to issue instructions in the government. Here too we can gradually nurture this habit. And the life span of a bouquet is very short. You receive it in your hand for a moment and then abandon it. But when you present a book, it becomes a part of the household, a part of the family.[11]

The story of India cannot be comprehended in its entirety without an appreciation of its spectrum of languages and dialects. Championing the primal role of native tongues, *Mann Ki Baat* has reinforced the importance of reading and learning while

---

[11]'PM's "Mann ki Baat" Programme on All India Radio', *PMIndia*, 25 June 2017, https://tinyurl.com/yc3m82ff. Accessed on 14 April 2023.

celebrating the many writers, poets and their great works of poetry and literature. A lifelong seeker of knowledge, PM Modi's dialogue with India is his quest to learn ever more from the best and finest minds of India.

CHAPTER 15

A PLATFORM FOR PEOPLE'S POWER

The making of each episode of *Mann Ki Baat* is an effort of unsung broadcast staff, editors, engineers and crowdsourcing analysts, all working in tandem with PM Modi as the episode goes from ideas to script concepts; from recording to transcription; followed by translation into multiple languages and dialects. While the episodes are delivered on the last Sunday of every month at the designated time slot of 11.00 a.m., the work related to *Mann Ki Baat* is a continuous process throughout the month, with important tasks, such as scrutinizing daily mails and letters, replying to queries and undertaking various correspondences, being performed on a daily basis.

ACTION BEFORE THE REVOLUTION

The process commences with the PM inviting suggestions for that month's *Mann Ki Baat* on MyGov web portal and NaMo app every month. MyGov platform, which has its origins in digital volunteering, is a cornerstone of the use of technology to crowdsource inputs over the years. By harnessing the power of the Internet, PM Modi has turned digital platforms into force multipliers to carry the message of *Mann Ki Baat* and also turned them into avenues for engaging volunteers, grassroots champions and entire communities digitally.

If the volume of physical letters received by the AIR is one measure of the popularity of old school radio, the multitudes of digital inputs through Twitter, Facebook, Instagram and the NaMo app are an indicator of how the Indian democracy is in action at the grassroots:

> Every time before Mann Ki Baat, letters are received from people; people share their ideas and viewpoints on Mygov and Narendra Modi Mobile App and there is also a toll-free number: 1800117800; and by calling on this number, people record messages in their own voice. My effort is that I read the maximum number of these letters and comments myself before Mann Ki Baat. I listen to many phone calls too. And as the episode of Mann Ki Baat draws closer, I read ideas and inputs sent by you very minutely while travelling.[1]

But these are more than just ideas, as revealed by the PM:

> These lakhs of letters did teach me something more. I became aware of very minute problems associated with governance. I would like to congratulate Akashvani for not treating these suggestions as mere bits of paper but considered them as

---

[1] 'PM's Address in 50th episode of Mann Ki Baat', *PMIndia*, 25 November 2018, https://tinyurl.com/mr2c42ya. Accessed on 13 April 2023.

expectations of the people. They conducted programmes after that. They called in various departments and put across to them the issues that the people had raised. They tried to get certain problems resolved. The various departments of the government analyzed these letters and segregated them as the ones related to policy matters, others to personal issues, some others as pointers that the government was not even aware of. Many things arose from the grass root level and reached the government. It is true, the basic principle of governance is that information should percolate upwards from bottom and guidance should percolate from the top to the bottom. Who would have thought that Mann Ki Baat will become a source of information? But this has happened.[2]

The steady use of technology through the nine years has seen the advent of telephonic inputs through an interactive voice response facility and a missed-call facility , along with the ability to listen to *Mann Ki Baat* in the language of choice telephonically.

This time I thought of conducting a new experiment through Mann Ki Baat. I had requested the citizens to call up telephonically and get their suggestions or queries recorded. I told them that I will take it up in Mann Ki Baat. I am happy that we received more than 55,000 calls from across the country—be it Siachen, Kutch or Kamrup, be it Kashmir or Kanyakumari. There is no part of India from which I did not receive a phone call. This is a pleasant experience in itself. People of all age groups have sent messages. I listened

[2]"English Rendering of Text of Prime Minister's "Mann Ki Baat" on All India Radio on 20th September 2015', *PMIndia*, 20 September 2015, https://tinyurl.com/36xan6ys. Accessed on 13 April 2023.

to some message personally and I liked them. My team is working on the others. You must have spent just a minute or two but for me your phone calls are very important. The entire government will work on your suggestions.

But there was something which surprised me and made me equally happy. These 55,000 people expressed themselves in their own way. It was frank interaction where they could say anything but I am surprised that all the things were in the shadow of Mann Ki Baat. They were totally positive, suggestion oriented and constructive. Just see how the citizens of the country are moving with a positive attitude, this is the nation's greatest wealth. There were serious complaints in about 1–2% phone calls. But more than 90% things were energizing and pleasant.[3]

The call for suggestions has different formats and flavours every month, with the recording and production of promotional audio and video by the twin teams of the AIR and Doordarshan. The promotional audio and video communicate all the details regarding the channels, day, date and time of broadcast for all the language versions, including the original broadcast.

The regularity and the discipline with which the recording of *Mann Ki Baat* takes place amidst the hectic schedule of the PM is symbolic of the manner in which the highest office operates. In the week preceding the broadcast, the AIR team follows a fixed itinerary to liaison with PM Modi's team to finalize the recording schedule. A dedicated team of production and engineering staff that have developed the *Mann Ki Baat* programme over the past nine years are put on a duty roster to ensure a flawless recording,

---

[3]Ibid.

with equipment checks and technical readiness undertaken in the studios prior to recording. It is fascinating that in spite of several advances in technology, the AIR's sound engineers and production staff rely on good old intuition to select the best quality audio recording from among three independent recording sources—digital, lapel and dynamic. While the transcription of the final recording are done simultaneously, the audio production gives final touches consistent with broadcast best practices for the radio broadcast.

Manohar Singh Rawat, assistant director of programme at the AIR, recalls his experience of working behind the scenes:

> I was immensely proud of having gotten the responsibility of producing the first episode of Mann Ki Baat. It was a matter of pride not only for me but also for entire AIR. With great power comes greater responsibility. As new and exciting it was, we knew that there is no margin for errors. After all, this is going to be a direct communication between people and the PM of largest democracy in the world. Given the stakes, I was nervous only till the first episode. It was the PM himself who created such atmosphere in that recording room which made every person comfortable and confident to deliver his best. It is because of him and his energy that I actively look forward to be part of every MKB episode devoid of any personal tragedies and thankfully have not missed since.[4]

His colleague Shaktidhar Dhyani, senior engineering assistant, was both excited and nervous during the first episode, knowing that the PM was going to be there. He says:

---

[4]In conversation with the author in March 2023.

I got to mike the PM! I still have that picture with me. He asked if the sound is okay and if there are any disturbances. I was pleasantly surprised by the amount of knowledge about audio systems he had. He listened to the whole recording patiently after we completed recording and gave us go ahead. I was very content witnessing the overall persona of our PM.[5]

Once both the final transcript and the accompanying audio product are available in broadcast-worthy quality, the creation of the video for *Mann Ki Baat* begins in earnest. A dedicated Doordarshan team then assembles the required visuals to go along with the script. As India's first and most widely viewed visual radio programme, *Mann Ki Baat* has set a high benchmark for having an innovative content format that integrates audio with video, adapting it for radio, TV and digital platforms. After Doordarshan has overlaid the relevant visuals over the audio of *Mann Ki Baat*, the visual radio version is ready for simulcast over TV and digital platforms, alongside the radio broadcast. Enriching of the visuals with on-ground footage is done by Doordarshan News teams, which fan out across India to put spotlight on the communities and grassroots champions highlighted by PM Modi in each episode of *Mann Ki Baat*.

A key element of the programme is its near real-time availability in more than 20 Indian languages (apart from English) and as many as 29 local dialects across India. To achieve the same, after the completion of the final version, audio and transcription of the episode are forwarded to radio and TV units across India for translation in the respective local languages and for subsequent visual adaptation. The Hindi transcription is translated into the

---

[5]Ibid.

local language and then recording takes place with an appropriate voiceover in that language.

According to Pramod Kumar, programme executive of *Mann Ki Baat*, 'It is a testament to our PM's oratory skills that makes *Mann Ki Baat* such a popular radio show which is running successfully in more than 20 Indian and 12 foreign languages.' He insists that the programme has not only helped the AIR enhance its reputation but has also made him a more responsible and dedicated employee. He adds, 'To produce every episode of *Mann Ki Baat*, there a lot of coordination between various departments that needs to happen. It gives an insight into the different dimensions of development that occur in our country, while showcasing the immense popularity the PM enjoys among the people. I eagerly wait for the next episode after finishing the current one.'[6]

Finally, the teams across India are all set for the broadcast day, that is, the last Sunday of the month. On this day, by 9.30 a.m., a final listening preview is done to ensure all pre-broadcast norms have been complied with and best practices have been followed. Immediately after the PM's broadcast, the regional versions are broadcast by the AIR and Doordarshan. The broadcast is also live-streamed on the AIR's official YouTube Channel and the NewsOnAir app. The same is the case with the multiple language versions.

Bhagwati Charan Baukhanti, who was one of the earliest personnel to transcribe *Mann Ki Baat* from its inception, was told that it would be broadcast as a scroll on Doordarshan and based on his write-up, many regional language transcriptions would be prepared. 'Although it was challenging in the beginning,

[6]Ibid.

the sheer value it held motivated me to study the PM's speeches, presentation, modulation, articulation and delivery. This helped me to get the subtle nuances like comma, interjection, punctuation, etc. exactly right,' he recalls. He adds, 'It's a fine opportunity for anyone to be a part of something as big as this and that's why I finish every episode with a lot of passion and integrity.'[7]

HARNESSING THE REAL POWER

The day after the broadcast, the recording and text of Hindi, English and Sanskrit versions are forwarded to Prasar Bharati Archives, along with all the other languages and dialects, for curation and compilation on *Mann Ki Baat*'s YouTube channel as language- and dialect-wise playlists, where all episodes may be found.

The many languages in which *Mann Ki Baat* is broadcast have resulted in the creation of a unique repository of multilingual content, representative of the diverse national character of India. This comprehensive digital repository comprises audio, video and transcripts in more than 40 languages and dialects, all easily accessible through the web on YouTube and multiple mobile applications. This textual repository of content in more than 20 Indian languages has inspired research in AI and natural language processing, leading to the development and refinement of language models and related algorithms. An interesting collaboration between researchers of the International Institute of Information Technology, Hyderabad (IIITH) and IIT Kanpur saw the use of *Mann Ki Baat* as a multilingual test set in Indian languages to establish a baseline for translation of Indian languages leveraging

---

[7]Ibid.

neural machine translation technology. The day is not far when we will perhaps witness AI-based applications further enriching and transforming the *Mann Ki Baat* experience for listeners and viewers across the globe transcending all barriers of distance and language.

The task of amplification of all the news and information related to the programme is carried out by the social media handles of the AIR and Doordarshan. They highlight anecdotes and media reports on the impact of *Mann Ki Baat* on societal change initiatives, and also share the experiences of the various change-makers and grassroots champions highlighted by the PM. The regional stations promote the broadcast in their regional languages. The programme also has a dedicated Twitter handle (@mannkibaat), which was started in July 2019.

Randhir Thakur, the programme executive at the AIR, who manages this dedicated Twitter handle insists that it is a significant responsibility. He says:

> In a way, you are like directly representing the PM himself. You are a 24x7 live interface between the PM and 1.3 billion people of this great country. There are personal joys too. It gives a feeling that I am contributing to society in some positive way. Second, the inspiring stories shared by the PM keep motivating you every single moment. I have read or gone through the stories of *Mann Ki Baat*, the maximum number of times. You have to post so many things on the handle that make you go through the episodes and stories countless number of times. In 2019, the official Twitter handle of *Mann Ki Baat* was launched. I have been associated with managing the Twitter handle every single day, curating content to be posted, making related graphics

and finally posting it. There is another way I'm associated with *Mann Ki Baat*. As everyone knows, it is also broadcast in multiple languages and dialects of India. Being the nodal person coordinating with regional stations for these regional versions, you have to be on your toes for the entire night verifying each of them. But all of these don't actually make you tired. On the contrary, it fills you with positivity and more energy and that to me is the real power of *Mann Ki Baat*.[8]

This aspect was also highlighted by the PM during the fiftieth episode:

Recently, All India Radio got a survey done on 'Mann Ki Baat'. I came across some feedback that is very interesting. Out of the designated sample in the survey, 70 per cent of respondents on an average happen to be listeners who regularly tune in to Mann Ki Baat. Most people believe that the greatest contribution of Mann Ki Baat has been the enhancement of a feeling of positivity in our society. The medium of Mann Ki Baat has promoted many a mass revolution. #indiapositive has been the subject of quite an extensive discussion. This is an exemplary glimpse of the feeling of positivity, innate to our countrymen. People have shared their experiences, conveying the rise of selfless volunteerism as a consequence of 'Mann Ki Baat'. It is a change where people are increasingly willing to contribute for the sake of service to society.[9]

---

[8]In conversation with the author in March 2023.
[9]'PM's Address in 50th episode of Mann Ki Baat', *PMIndia*, 25 November 2018, https://tinyurl.com/mr2c42ya. Accessed on 13 April 2023.

SUCCESS STORIES AND CASE STUDIES

Mann Ki Baat has inspired both individuals and institutions alike to make societal change not just a mass movement but a way of life. From personal stories of individual efforts to institutional change initiatives, the impact of *Mann Ki Baat* has been visible across India over the past nine years.

There are several instances of citizen action, ranging from a bicycle rally in Gujarat, aimed at generating awareness on energy conservation, to the building of a check dam in nine days in Madhya Pradesh for water conservation. Such has been the motivation that urban and rural India alike have risen to the occasion to do their bit in public and national interest.

The IIT Madras saw its alumni association launch Mission Million Smiles—an initiative to create a positive impact on the lives of at least one million people in India and the rest of the world in two years—by seeking to channelize the energy, resources and commitment of its alumni members. Inspired by PM Modi's address on the importance of alumni associations to the nation, the IIT Madras association committed itself to undertaking multiple change initiatives.

The programme has also infused raw enthusiasm and zeal among the youth of India, and has encouraged them to become change agents. Kendriya Vidyalaya, Ballygunge, Kolkata, is a good example of how children became foot soldiers of the cleanliness drive underlying the Swachh Bharat Abhiyan. Nestled inside Ballygunge Military Camp, the school has been the site of classroom and campus cleaning, with students and teachers participating at least once at the end of every month. Encouraged by listening to *Mann Ki Baat*, student committees in every class, headed by a nominated prefect, have taken on the ownership of cleanliness and hygiene setting an example for the society at large.

The effectiveness of *Mann Ki Baat* for mass outreach has been validated by several studies. One such study involved eight focus group discussions in rural parts of two blocks of Ghaziabad district and two blocks of Muzaffarnagar district, Uttar Pradesh.[10] The study analysed the accessibility and availability of various communication channels and mediums, commonly utilized by community groups targeted in efforts to eradicate open defecation. Interestingly, all respondents immediately recalled hearing the PM's message regarding open defecation on TV during commercial breaks and his *Mann Ki Baat* programme. A few male respondents, old and young people, also correlated the PM's messages to billboard advertisements they had seen in the district headquarters or cities. The extent to which *Mann Ki Baat* may have influenced behavioural change in the effort to eliminate open defecation can be gauged from instances such as these.

While khadi sales have seen a significant boost after PM Modi's call to action, it has also inspired experiments in rural India to leverage handloom weaving as an entrepreneurial tool for women SHGs. A study published in the *International Journal of Education and Management Studies* in 2020 describes how SHGs located in two villages, Dhangar and Bighar in the Fatehabad district of Haryana, saw women being imparted skills training in handloom weaving to spur entrepreneurial

---

[10]Gupta, Deepak and Agarwal, Anusha, 'Open Defecation—A Behaviour Change Communication Challenge | India on the Move', *Communication: Achieving Results for Children*, 9 May 2017, https://tinyurl.com/59scdxts. Accessed on 13 April 2023.

activity in the villages, inspired by PM Modi's *Mann Ki Baat*.[11]

So how exactly has PM Modi been so effective at using *Mann Ki Baat* to inspire?

The answer perhaps lies in his use of motivational language. According to a study published in the October 2021 edition of *Asian Politics & Policy*, PM Modi's use of empathetic language that offers guidance and encourages people to take actions, while also imparting a greater sense of meaning and purpose, contributes significantly to the radio programme's effectiveness.[12] The study entailed a survey of students in Jaipur making use of formal constructs of motivational language theory through a questionnaire. The survey also assessed the effectiveness of PM Modi as a leader and as a storyteller, employing *Mann Ki Baat* as a tool.

Perhaps the greatest contribution of *Mann Ki Baat* has been consistently reinforcing positive thinking. An objective measure of the same was revealed by a study on topic modelling extraction of *Mann Ki Baat* using textual analytics, published in the *European Journal of Mathematics and Statistics* in its January 2021 edition.[13] A total of 60 episodes (October 2014 to December 2019) of *Mann Ki Baat*, gathered from *PMindia* website were analysed in detail. Frequently used terms and recurring topics were determined and analysed in this study by researchers from the Department of

[11]Dahiya, Rajesh, and Yadav, Saroj, 'Handloom Weaving: An Entrepreneurial Tool for SHG Women', *International Journal of Education and Management Studies*, Vol. 10, No. 2, 2020, pp. 186–90.

[12]Sharma, Daneshwar and Dubey, Akash D., 'The Political Leader's Motivating Language Use and His Perceived Effectiveness: The Case of Narendra Modi's *Mann Ki Baat*', *Asian Politics & Policy*, Vol. 13, No. 4, 2021, pp. 534–53.

[13]Kandukuri, Mounika and HaraGopal, V.V. 'Topic Modelling Extraction of "Mann Ki Baat"', *European Journal of Mathematics and Statistics*, Vol. 2, No. 1, 2021, pp. 1–12.

Statistics, University College of Science, Osmania University in Hyderabad and the Department of Mathematics, Birla Institute of Technology and Science (BITS) in Pilani. Assessing positivity in the underlying message of *Mann Ki Baat*, the study revealed high-frequency topics such as achievements and works of historical leaders and freedom fighters; initiatives like Fit India; importance of yoga; wellness awareness for enhancing health and quality of life; stress-free approaches for students appearing for exams; and themes such as social life, public life, lifestyle, cleanliness and environmental conservation.

The ability of *Mann Ki Baat* to initiate change in the minds of citizens across India was the subject of a study presented at 7th International Conference on Information Technology and Quality Management, 2019.[14] The study conducted by researchers from the Department of Humanities and Social Sciences at BITS Pilani, K K Birla Goa Campus, and the Goa Institute of Management found that positive sentiments dominated *Mann Ki Baat*, while more than 14 per cent of the language used reinforced trust in the citizens. Sharing joy and building a sense of anticipation dominated negative sentiments of sadness or anger.

A WARM, APOLITICAL PLATFORM

The apolitical character of *Mann Ki Baat* has, in many ways, added to the overall effectiveness of its outreach to citizens, irrespective of political leanings or affiliations despite repeated

[14]Upadhyay, Shalini and Upadhyay, Nitin, 'Investigating Prime Minister Narendra Modi's Usage of Pathos in the Cyber-Physical Society—A Case of Public Relations Campaign', *Procedia Computer Science*, Vol. 162, 2009, pp. 400–04.

calls by the political opposition to discuss hot-button political issues on the programme. As the PM says:

> When 'Mann Ki Baat' commenced, I had firmly decided that it would carry nothing political, or any praise for the Government, nor Modi for that matter anywhere. The greatest bulwark in ensuring adherence to my resolve; in fact, my highest inspiration, has been YOU. As a run up to each episode of 'Mann Ki Baat', the expectations and aspirations of listeners through their letters, online comments and phone calls are crystal clear. Modi may come and go, but this country will never let go of its unity and permanence, our culture will always be immortal. These minute stories encompassing 130 crore countrymen will always stay alive. This new inspiration and zest will keep taking her to greater heights.[15]

This apolitical character was the subject of a study by researchers from the Indian Institute of Management, Indore, in 2019.[16] The analysis was based on 53 episodes of *Mann Ki Baat* that aired between October 2014 and February 2019. Its findings offered a glimpse into how PM Modi preserved the apolitical character of *Mann Ki Baat*. While the researchers looked for ideological subjects and personalities within *Mann Ki Baat*, the findings reveal how references to three national icons—Mahatma Gandhi, Dr B.R. Ambedkar and Sardar Vallabhbhai Patel—have dominated *Mann Ki Baat* by a wide margin. If *Mann Ki Baat*

---

[15]'PM's Address in 50th episode of Mann Ki Baat', *PMIndia*, 25 November 2018, https://tinyurl.com/mr2c42ya. Accessed on 13 April 2023.
[16]Jayaprakash, R., '"Mann Ki Baat" Is India's Biggest Online Influencer', *The Sunday Guardian*, 29 June 2019, https://tinyurl.com/28umha4c. Accessed on 13 April 2023.

has emerged as the mass movement that it is today, the role of these icons of India as symbols of grassroots change cannot be understated.

An in-depth analysis of how PM Modi established a personal connect is revealed by Jean-Thomas Martelli.[17] The study finds extensive use of lexicon that seeks to establish a direct personal connect with the citizens through disintermediation. Intimacy and simplicity of communication, according to the study, help *Mann Ki Baat* in conveying key messages of social change through everyday relatable stories invoking closeness, kinship and personal warmth. The conclusions highlight a pertinent point on what *Mann Ki Baat* has come to mean to more than 100 crore Indians—a warm, apolitical platform for promoting hope and motivating self-betterment through a deeply personal and national ethos of *seva* or service.

> Mann Ki Baat became a platform to express the power of society. I had just casually mentioned about selfie with daughter and what a movement it became. The whole world was amazed. Lakhs of people, perhaps from all the countries of the world posted a selfie with their daughters. What dignity did it lend to our daughters? Anyone who clicked this selfie not only boosted their daughter's confidence but also made a commitment to themselves. Whosoever saw it realized that they will now have to give up the indifferent attitude towards daughters. This was a kind of a silent revolution.
>
> I had casually mentioned to my fellow citizens, keeping

---

[17]'Guru ki Baat: Populism and Connect in Modi's Mann ki Baats', *Jean-Thomas Martelli*, 21 November 2020, https://tinyurl.com/2tsh86ha. Accessed on 13 April 2023.

in mind the tourism industry of India to send me good pictures of the destination they travel to on the lines of Incredible India so that I can also see them. People sent pictures in lakhs from every corner of India. Neither the Government of India nor the state tourism departments were aware of such heritage. All things were brought together on a platform and the government did not have to spend a single penny. The people themselves took the task forward.

In October last year, I did my first "Mann Ki Baat". In that edition I had mentioned about Gandhi Jayanti. I told people that we are celebrating Gandhiji's birth Anniversary on 2nd October. There was a time when there was Khadi for Nation? Isn't it the need of the hour that there be Khadi for fashion? I requested the people to buy Khadi and to do their bit. Today, I can say with great satisfaction that in the past one year the sales of Khadi have almost doubled. Now see, there was no government advertisement. Nor were lakhs and crores spent. A simple feeling and realization by the people have brought this change.

Once I had mentioned in "Mann Ki Baat" about the problem of poor families, how their children cry due to the pollution when the wooden stove is lit. Shouldn't they be getting gas cylinders? And I had requested the affluent to surrender their gas subsidy. Just think... today I can say with great pride that 30 lakh families have given up their gas subsidy and these are not the rich people. I saw on T.V, a retired teacher, a widow lady standing in a queue to give up her subsidy. The common people from the society belonging to the middle and lower middle class have difficulty in giving up subsidy. But then they did give up their subsidy. Isn't it a silent revolution? Isn't it a demonstration of the people's power?[18]

This silent revolution was the focus of a study sponsored by the Bill & Melinda Gates Foundation. The study conducted by the Institute for Competitiveness (IFC), with research support from Axis My India, found that *Mann Ki Baat* stood out as a unique initiative led by any political leader that celebrated people's resolve and action to bring about societal change and transformation.[19] The study also highlighted a survey by the Indian Institute of Management Rohtak, which surveyed over 10,000 respondents across India to study the outreach of *Mann Ki Baat*.[20] While this survey estimated that over a hundred crore listeners have been touched by the radio programme, the IFC study has revealed how *Mann Ki Baat* has catalysed collective action towards achieving Sustainable Development Goals (SDGs) identified by the United Nations. According to the IFC study, a defining characteristic of this collective action has been the ability of *Mann Ki Baat* to reconnect people with traditional cultural values to spur societal change, from environmental sensitivity to water conservation. With *Mann Ki Baat*'s wide-ranging impact on all 17 of the SDGs, it is no surprise that the director-general of the UNESCO, Audrey Azoulay, in conversation with PM Modi during the hundredth

[18]'English Rendering of Text of Prime Minister's "Mann Ki Baat" on All India Radio on 20th September 2015', *PMIndia*, 20 September 2015, https://tinyurl.com/36xan6ys. Accessed on 13 April 2023.
[19]'Mann ki Baat: A Decade of Reflections', *Institute for Competitiveness*, 28 April 2023, https://tinyurl.com/ytmzap7s. Accessed on 1 May 2023.
[20]'Ahead of 100th Episode, IIM Survey Finds Mann Ki Baat Has Reached 100 Crore Listeners', *Press Information Bureau*, 24 April 2023, https://tinyurl.com/3wmhjp8a. Accessed on 1 May 2023.

episode of *Mann Ki Baat*, focussed on the uniquely Indian way in which culture has been blended with education on the road to achieving these goals.[21] From a study by the Indian Institute of Mass Communication to the research presented in *Journal of Research in Ayurvedic Sciences*, the confluence of traditions, culture and education becomes abundantly clear in the manner in which *Mann Ki Baat* has influenced India, its people and communities.[22]

It is this collective spirit that has resulted in concrete action. Who better than PM Modi to summarize the true essence of *Mann Ki Baat*:

> My countrymen stay in my heart every moment and that is how the writer's situation and ideas expressed in the letter become part of my thought process. That letter does not remain a mere a piece of paper for me. As it is I have spent close to 40 to 45 years as a travelling mendicant and have been to most of the districts in our country including the remotest once where I spent a lot of time. That is why I am able to relate myself to the place and context of the letter. Then, I note down facts like the name of the village and of the person. Honestly speaking, Mann Ki Baat carries my voice but the examples, emotions and spirit represent my countrymen.
>
> I thank every person contributing to Mann Ki Baat.

---

[21]'PM's Address in the 100th Episode of "Mann Ki Baat"', *PMIndia*, 30 April 2023, https://tinyurl.com/378fbvdy. Accessed on 1 May 2023.

[22]'"Mann ki Baat" Connects India to Bharat', *Press Information Bureau*, 29 April 2023, https://tinyurl.com/4vduteuh. Accessed on 1 May 2023; '"Mann ki Baat" Conversations Have Been Instrumental in Giving a Positive Trust to Ayush: Shri Sarbananda Sonowal', *Press Information Bureau*, 28 April 2023, https://tinyurl.com/yc2sr9u6. Accessed on 1 May 2023.

There are lakhs of persons whose names I have not been able to include in Mann Ki Baat but without any disappointment, they continue to send in their letters and comments. I firmly believe that your ideas and your views will continue reaching me in even greater numbers and will help make Mann Ki Baat more interesting, effective and useful.[23]

---

[23]'PM's Address in 50th episode of Mann Ki Baat', *PMIndia*, 25 November 2018, https://tinyurl.com/mr2c42ya. Accessed on 13 April 2023.

ANNEXURE 1

YOUTUBE PLAYLISTS OF RADIO BROADCASTS OF *MANN KI BAAT* IN 39 INDIAN LANGUAGES AND DIALECTS

Sr. No.	Language	YouTube Link	QR Code
1	Adi	https://www.youtube.com/playlist?list=PLCBw-fFXg4R2Pgi6G_0Y4RMa1XZkOMVHe	
2	Gondi	https://www.youtube.com/playlist?list=PLCBw-fFXg4R1c3HyW3KDAQM0GzsxZWzQH	
3	Halbi	https://www.youtube.com/playlist?list=PLCBw-fFXg4R1AMgGkD0I6-ekYC7iyfMEe	
4	Lepcha	https://www.youtube.com/playlist?list=PLCBw-fFXg4R0C1AHGfIwnDvOM7nz9XE_e	

5	Garo	https://www.youtube.com/playlist?list=PLCBw-fFXg4R1_EYp_vL4cDXJMe1T8FjHV	
6	Kashmiri	https://www.youtube.com/playlist?list=PLCBw-fFXg4R2QS-So_2G_RvaTjqwxL9se	
7	Telugu	https://www.youtube.com/playlist?list=PLCBw-fFXg4R14Odhf1k121R24gYCw2o0y	
8	Marathi	https://www.youtube.com/playlist?list=PLCBw-fFXg4R1VpjojM7a0RYZq04X_CVuJ	
9	Kannada	https://www.youtube.com/playlist?list=PLCBw-fFXg4R3qxxhewDFMCK2zRMadOjn9	
10	Dogri	https://www.youtube.com/playlist?list=PLCBw-fFXg4R1phxMRr8bMQGNbCJ2CKiF3	
11	Tamil	https://www.youtube.com/playlist?list=PLCBw-fFXg4R2VOMhGRNc4q2wDhMACqdLj	
12	Assamese	https://www.youtube.com/playlist?list=PLCBw-fFXg4R1saY2lQhiiBlXmpEZCHzUs	
13	Khasi	https://www.youtube.com/playlist?list=PLCBw-fFXg4R3AqG4SIu2qRQ-IoUHV_V3E	
14	Nepali	https://www.youtube.com/playlist?list=PLCBw-fFXg4R1UaOt78FJK0HTrEgdSECBh	

15	Maithili	https://www.youtube.com/playlist?list=PLCBw-fFXg4R2IlqIjTSq8fjpOL-AeIVBM	
16	Santhali	https://www.youtube.com/playlist?list=PLCBw-fFXg4R1RSJi0OK3MlRkbQbniGZlZ	
17	Bengali	https://www.youtube.com/playlist?list=PLCBw-fFXg4R1cCY_cG2AEgwZz72smLU-Z	
18	Bodo	https://www.youtube.com/playlist?list=PLCBw-fFXg4R212_ZPpffptyaOvaFdEZVc	
19	Punjabi	https://www.youtube.com/playlist?list=PLCBw-fFXg4R11HJjSoU_yyFwwTt3q_RKe	
20	Jaintia	https://www.youtube.com/playlist?list=PLCBw-fFXg4R2jKbJ3Lk5mBFXwPBuheagj	
21	Manipuri	https://www.youtube.com/playlist?list=PLCBw-fFXg4R02s6hYASCnBPx4luFP3dJq	
22	Sign Language	https://www.youtube.com/playlist?list=PLCBw-fFXg4R3yGyQOrGljZ8w0LfYSMKad	
23	Purgi	https://www.youtube.com/playlist?list=PLCBw-fFXg4R0yQTfiJ9jdPxMitcQffvvL	
24	Sikkimese	https://www.youtube.com/playlist?list=PLCBw-fFXg4R3Mtiyl1pOiPsNP-9Vchftl	

25	Urdu	https://www.youtube.com/playlist?list=PLCBw-fFXg4R07KilvSz6s7041yAjmgWgF	
26	Sindhi	https://www.youtube.com/playlist?list=PLCBw-fFXg4R3cEkLDbjPBRc3QYJ9Da8Hj	
27	Odia	https://www.youtube.com/playlist?list=PLCBw-fFXg4R1Vvq3SM-Str8ACeW_UxNw6	
28	Mizo	https://www.youtube.com/playlist?list=PLCBw-fFXg4R1opRqid1b3uyvfXpGTw0zA	
29	Konkani	https://www.youtube.com/playlist?list=PLCBw-fFXg4R2WjuGHX43HH-XB0Y5EROni	
30	Chhattis-garhi	https://www.youtube.com/playlist?list=PLCBw-fFXg4R1KsgudFgHkgiiCF7hSsDDI	
31	Sanskrit	https://www.youtube.com/playlist?list=PLCBw-fFXg4R1i1QK4qsT5hu1bKvExu7TL	
32	Malayalam	https://www.youtube.com/playlist?list=PLCBw-fFXg4R1FVYrSlYnZN2mXgvYVtMH4	
33	English	https://www.youtube.com/playlist?list=PLCBw-fFXg4R21CXTxNRi_rQkj3VNuu6n6	
34	Gujarati	https://www.youtube.com/playlist?list=PLCBw-fFXg4R2jXJTF17wBYRUwQL_xpM9U	

35	Ladakhi	https://www.youtube.com/playlist?list=PLCBw-fFXg4R08z6pTAWMpRFMrAjJM75kf	
36	Sargujiha	https://www.youtube.com/playlist?list=PLCBw-fFXg4R2yguJ5ZVTPCHRz6Xis4Rpw	
37	Nyishi	https://www.youtube.com/playlist?list=PLCBw-fFXg4R1tR4rGWBK-rYr5G7B--tu9	
38	Hindi (1.0)	https://www.youtube.com/playlist?list=PLspw0meV6Wr5TUAjb-KO414VlEkVPD0IU	
39	Hindi (2.0)	https://www.youtube.com/playlist?list=PLspw0meV6Wr4dTQ9wuxY4ZjjJYuCYxdXY	

MANN *KI BAAT* REGIONAL-LANGUAGE VERSIONS FOR TV BROADCAST

Sr. No.	Language	Link
1.	Tamil	https://www.youtube.com/@
2.	Telugu	prasarbharati7282/playlists
3.	Malayalam	
4.	Kannada	
5.	Odia	
6.	Bengali	
7.	Gujarati	
8.	Marathi	
9.	Chhattisgarhi	
10.	Kashmiri	
11.	Dogri	
12.	Khasi	
13.	Manipuri	
14.	Assamese	
15.	Punjabi	
16.	Sign Language	

ANNEXURE 3

ENGLISH TRANSLATION OF THE TEXT OF *MANN KI BAAT* EPISODES

Episode Number	Episode Link	QR Code
1	https://www.pmindia.gov.in/en/news_updates/english-rendering-of-the-text-of-pms-first-address-to-the-nation-on-radio/	
2	https://www.pmindia.gov.in/en/news_updates/english-rendering-of-text-of-prime-ministers-mann-ki-baat-on-all-india-radio/	
3	https://www.pmindia.gov.in/en/news_updates/english-rendering-of-the-text-of-prime-ministers-mann-ki-baat-on-all-india-radio-on-14th-december-2014/	
4	https://www.pmindia.gov.in/en/news_updates/english-rendering-of-transcript-of-the-special-episode-of-mann-ki-baat-pm-shri-narendra-modi-and-us-president-shri-barack-obama-share-their-thoughts-on-radio/	

5	https://www.pmindia.gov.in/en/news_updates/english-rendering-of-text-of-prime-ministers-mann-ki-baat-on-all-india-radio-in-february-2015/	
6	https://www.pmindia.gov.in/en/news_updates/english-rendering-of-pms-mann-ki-baat-address-on-all-india-radio/	
7	https://www.pmindia.gov.in/en/news_updates/english-rendering-of-text-of-prime-ministers-mann-ki-baat-on-all-india-radio-on-26th-april-2015/	
8	https://www.pmindia.gov.in/en/news_updates/english-rendering-of-the-text-of-prime-minister-shri-narendra-modis-address-to-the-nation-on-all-india-radio/	
9	https://www.pmindia.gov.in/en/news_updates/english-rendering-of-prime-ministers-mann-ki-baat-address-on-all-india-radio/	
10	https://www.pmindia.gov.in/en/news_updates/english-rendering-of-prime-ministers-mann-ki-baat-on-all-india-radio/	
11	https://www.pmindia.gov.in/en/news_updates/english-rendering-of-pms-mann-ki-baat-on-all-india-radio/	
12	https://www.pmindia.gov.in/en/news_updates/english-rendering-of-text-of-prime-ministers-mann-ki-baat-on-all-india-radio-on-20th-september-2015/	
13	https://www.pmindia.gov.in/en/news_updates/english-rendering-of-pms-mann-ki-baat-on-all-india-radio-on-october-2015/	

14	https://www.pmindia.gov.in/en/news_updates/ english-rendering-of-prime-ministers-mann-ki-baat-on-all-india-radio-29th-november-2015/	
15	https://www.pmindia.gov.in/en/news_updates/ english-rendering-text-of-pms-mann-ki-baat-on-all-india-radio-on-27-12-2015/	
16	https://www.pmindia.gov.in/en/news_updates/ text-of-prime-ministers-mann-ki-baat-on-all-india-radio-8/	
17	https://www.pmindia.gov.in/en/news_updates/ text-of-prime-ministers-mann-ki-baat-on-all-india-radio-9/	
18	https://www.pmindia.gov.in/en/news_updates/text-of-pms-mann-ki-baat-programme-on-all-india-radio-2/	
19	https://www.pmindia.gov.in/en/news_updates/pms-mann-ki-baat-programme-at-all-india-radio/	
20	https://www.pmindia.gov.in/en/news_updates/text-of-pms-mann-ki-baatprogramme-on-all-india-radio-on-22-05-2016/	
21	https://www.pmindia.gov.in/en/news_updates/pms-mann-ki-baat-programme-on-all-india-radio-on-june-26-2016/	
22	https://www.pmindia.gov.in/en/news_updates/pms-mann-ki-baat-programme-on-all-india-radio/	
23	https://www.pmindia.gov.in/en/news_updates/pms-mann-ki-baat-programme-on-all-india-radio-on-august-28-2016/	

24	https://www.pmindia.gov.in/en/news_updates/text-of-pms-mann-ki-baat-programme-on-all-india-radio-on-25-september-2016/	
25	https://www.pmindia.gov.in/en/news_updates/pms-mann-ki-baat-address-on-all-india-radio-on-30-october-2016/	
26	https://www.pmindia.gov.in/en/news_updates/pms-mann-ki-baat-address-on-all-india-radio/	
27	https://www.pmindia.gov.in/en/news_updates/pms-mann-ki-baat-address-on-all-india-radio-2/	
28	https://www.pmindia.gov.in/en/news_updates/pms-mann-ki-baat-address-on-all-india-radio-3/	
29	https://www.pmindia.gov.in/en/news_updates/pms-mann-ki-baat-address-on-all-india-radio-4/	
30	https://www.pmindia.gov.in/en/news_updates/text-of-pms-mann-ki-baat-programme-on-all-india-radio-3/	
31	https://www.pmindia.gov.in/en/news_updates/english-rendering-of-mann-ki-baat-address-by-pm-on-all-india-radio/	
32	https://www.pmindia.gov.in/en/news_updates/pms-mann-ki-baat-programme-on-all-india-radio-2/	
33	https://www.pmindia.gov.in/en/news_updates/pms-mann-ki-baat-programme-on-all-india-radio-3/	

34	https://www.pmindia.gov.in/en/news_updates/pms-mann-ki-baat-programme-on-all-india-radio-4/	
35	https://www.pmindia.gov.in/en/news_updates/pms-mann-ki-baat-programme-on-all-india-radio-5/	
36	https://www.pmindia.gov.in/en/news_updates/pms-mann-ki-baat-programme-on-all-india-radio-6/	
37	https://www.pmindia.gov.in/en/news_updates/pms-mann-ki-baat-programme-on-all-india-radio-7/	
38	https://www.pmindia.gov.in/en/news_updates/pms-mann-ki-baat-programme-on-all-india-radio-8/	
39	https://www.pmindia.gov.in/en/news_updates/pms-mann-ki-baat-programme-on-all-india-radio-9/	
40	https://www.pmindia.gov.in/en/news_updates/pms-mann-ki-baat-programme-on-all-india-radio-10/	
41	https://www.pmindia.gov.in/en/news_updates/pms-mann-ki-baat-programme-on-all-india-radio-11/	
42	https://www.pmindia.gov.in/en/news_updates/pms-mann-ki-baat-programme-on-all-india-radio-12/	
43	https://www.pmindia.gov.in/en/news_updates/pms-mann-ki-baat-programme-on-all-india-radio-13/	

44	https://www.pmindia.gov.in/en/news_updates/pms-mann-ki-baat-programme-on-all-india-radio-14/	
45	https://www.pmindia.gov.in/en/news_updates/pms-mann-ki-baat-programme-on-all-india-radio-15/	
46	https://www.pmindia.gov.in/en/news_updates/pms-mann-ki-baat-programme-on-all-india-radio-16/	
47	https://www.pmindia.gov.in/en/news_updates/pms-mann-ki-baat-programme-on-all-india-radio-17/	
48	https://www.pmindia.gov.in/en/news_updates/pms-address-in-48th-episode-of-mann-ki-baat/	
49	https://www.pmindia.gov.in/en/news_updates/pms-mann-ki-baat-programme-on-all-india-radio-18/	
50	https://www.pmindia.gov.in/en/news_updates/pms-address-in-50th-episode-of-mann-ki-baat/	
51	https://www.pmindia.gov.in/en/news_updates/pms-mann-ki-baat-programme-on-all-india-radio-19/	
52	https://www.pmindia.gov.in/en/news_updates/pms-mann-ki-baat-programme-on-all-india-radio-20/	
53	https://www.pmindia.gov.in/en/news_updates/pms-mann-ki-baat-programme-on-all-india-radio-21/	

54	https://www.pmindia.gov.in/en/news_updates/pms-address-in-mann-ki-baat-2-0programme-on-all-india-radio/	
55	https://www.pmindia.gov.in/en/news_updates/pms-address-in-2nd-episode-of-mann-ki-baat-2-0/	
56	https://www.pmindia.gov.in/en/news_updates/pms-address-in-3rd-episode-of-mann-ki-baat-2-0/	
57	https://www.pmindia.gov.in/en/news_updates/pms-address-in-4th-episode-of-mann-ki-baat-2-0/	
58	https://www.pmindia.gov.in/en/news_updates/pms-address-in-the-5th-episode-of-mann-ki-baat-2-0/	
59	https://www.pmindia.gov.in/en/news_updates/pms-address-in-the-6th-episode-of-mann-ki-baat-2-0/	
60	https://www.pmindia.gov.in/en/news_updates/pms-address-in-the-7th-episode-of-mann-ki-baat-2-0/	
61	https://www.pmindia.gov.in/en/news_updates/pms-address-in-the-8th-episode-of-mann-ki-baat-2-0/	
62	https://www.pmindia.gov.in/en/news_updates/pms-address-in-the-9th-episode-of-mann-ki-baat-2-0/	
63	https://www.pmindia.gov.in/en/news_updates/pms-address-in-the-10th-episode-of-mann-ki-baat-2-0/	

64	https://www.pmindia.gov.in/en/news_updates/pms-address-in-the-11th-episode-of-mann-ki-baat-2-0/	
65	https://www.pmindia.gov.in/en/news_updates/pms-address-in-the-12th-episode-of-mann-ki-baat-2-0/	
66	https://www.pmindia.gov.in/en/news_updates/pms-address-in-the-13th-episode-of-mann-ki-baat-2-0/	
67	https://www.pmindia.gov.in/en/news_updates/pms-address-in-the-14th-episode-of-mann-ki-baat-2-0/	
68	https://www.pmindia.gov.in/en/news_updates/pms-address-in-the-15th-episode-of-mann-ki-baat-2-0/	
69	https://www.pmindia.gov.in/en/news_updates/pms-address-in-the-16th-episode-of-mann-ki-baat-2-0/	
70	https://www.pmindia.gov.in/en/news_updates/pms-address-in-the-17th-episode-of-mann-ki-baat-2-0/	
71	https://www.pmindia.gov.in/en/news_updates/pms-address-in-the-18th-episode-of-mann-ki-baat-2-0/	
72	https://www.pmindia.gov.in/en/news_updates/pms-address-in-the-19th-episode-of-mann-ki-baat-2-0/	
73	https://www.pmindia.gov.in/en/news_updates/pms-address-in-the-20th-episode-of-mann-ki-baat-2-0/	

74	https://www.pmindia.gov.in/en/news_updates/pms-address-in-the-21st-episode-of-mann-ki-baat-2-0/	
75	https://www.pmindia.gov.in/en/news_updates/pms-address-in-the-75thepisode-of-mann-ki-baat/	
76	https://www.pmindia.gov.in/en/news_updates/pms-address-in-the-76th-episode-of-mann-ki-baat/	
77	https://www.pmindia.gov.in/en/news_updates/pms-address-in-the-77th-episode-of-mann-ki-baat/	
78	https://www.pmindia.gov.in/en/news_updates/pms-address-in-the-78th-episode-of-mann-ki-baat/	
79	https://www.pmindia.gov.in/en/news_updates/pms-address-in-the-79th-episode-of-mann-ki-baat/	
80	https://www.pmindia.gov.in/en/news_updates/pms-address-in-the-80th-episode-of-mann-ki-baat/	
81	https://www.pmindia.gov.in/en/news_updates/pms-address-in-the-81st-episode-of-mann-ki-baat/	
82	https://www.pmindia.gov.in/en/news_updates/pms-address-in-the-82nd-episode-of-mann-ki-baat/	
83	https://www.pmindia.gov.in/en/news_updates/pms-address-in-the-83rd-episode-of-mann-ki-baat/	

84	https://www.pmindia.gov.in/en/news_updates/pms-address-in-the-84th-episode-of-mann-ki-baat/	
85	https://www.pmindia.gov.in/en/news_updates/pms-address-in-the-85th-episode-of-mann-ki-baat-on-30-01-2022/	
86	https://www.pmindia.gov.in/en/news_updates/pms-address-in-the-86th-episode-of-mann-ki-baat/	
87	https://www.pmindia.gov.in/en/news_updates/pms-address-in-the-87th-episode-of-mann-ki-baat/	
88	https://www.pmindia.gov.in/en/news_updates/pms-address-in-the-88th-episode-of-mann-ki-baat/	
89	https://www.pmindia.gov.in/en/news_updates/pms-address-in-the-89th-episode-of-mann-ki-baat/	
90	https://www.pmindia.gov.in/en/news_updates/pms-address-in-the-90th-episode-of-mann-ki-baat/	
91	https://www.pmindia.gov.in/en/news_updates/pms-address-in-the-91st-episode-of-mann-ki-baat/	
92	https://www.pmindia.gov.in/en/news_updates/pms-address-in-the-92nd-episode-of-mann-ki-baat/	
93	https://www.pmindia.gov.in/en/news_updates/pms-address-in-the-93rd-episode-of-mann-ki-baat/	

94	https://www.pmindia.gov.in/en/news_updates/pms-address-in-the-94th-episode-of-mann-ki-baat/	
95	https://www.pmindia.gov.in/en/news_updates/pms-address-in-the-95th-episode-of-mann-ki-baat/	
96	https://www.pmindia.gov.in/en/news_updates/pms-address-in-the-96th-episode-of-mann-ki-baat/	
97	https://www.pmindia.gov.in/en/news_updates/pms-address-in-the-97th-episode-of-mann-ki-baat/	
98	https://www.pmindia.gov.in/en/news_updates/pms-address-in-the-98th-episode-of-mann-ki-baat/	
99	https://www.pmindia.gov.in/en/news_updates/pms-address-in-the-99th-episode-of-mann-ki-baat/	

FOREIGN-LANGUAGE VERSIONS OF *MANN KI BAAT* BROADCAST BY EXTERNAL SERVICES DIVISION OF ALL INDIA RADIO

Sr. No	Foreign Languages
1.	Arabic
2.	Baluchi
3.	Chinese
4.	Dari
5.	Pashto
6.	Persian
7.	Swahili
8.	Indonesian
9.	Burmese
10.	Tibetan
11.	French

INDEX